Beating
Depression

Also available in this series

Asserting yourself
Coping with stress
Controlling your weight

BEATING
DEPRESSION

by Dr. John Rush

Illustrated by Mel Calman

Facts On File Publications

New York, New York • Oxford, England

BEATING DEPRESSION

Published by Facts On File, Inc., 460 Park Avenue South, New York, New York 10016.

First published by Century Publishing Co. Ltd., 76 Old Compton Street, London W1V 5PA.

Library of Congress Cataloging in Publication Data

Rush, John.
    Beating depression.

    (Pocket your problems)
    Bibliography: p.
    Includes index.
    1. Depression, Mental.   2. Cognitive therapy.
I. Title.   II. Series.
RC537.R87   1985   616.85'27   84-13564
ISBN 0-8160-1104-4

Printed in United States of America
10 9 8 7 6 5 4 3 2 1

Contents

Dedication

To my parents and my sister, without whose guidance, support and sacrifice this volume could not have been produced.

Introduction

Anyone who has suffered from depression knows that there are few worse conditions in the world. Many sufferers say they would rather have the most crippling illness there is than suffer depression. I have even heard some people say they would prefer cancer. The worst thing about depression is that it condemns one to a living death, with no pleasure or joy in the present or the foreseeable future.

That is why any book that gives more information about this horrible condition is welcome. Dr Rush very clearly explains the different types of depression, how they arise and how they are treated. It is very important to know what treatment is available because the first dose of pills or the first sessions of therapy do not always lift the depression. That may not happen until many different remedies have been tried.

I would not write so vehemently about depression if I had not suffered from it myself. Over the years of my depression I saw life passing by through an emotional plate-glass window. Even with friends I felt unable to make contact, isolated, different, incapable of experiencing pleasure as they did. I remember waking each morning and asking myself 'Would you like to die today?' and answering 'I only wish I could'. Perhaps what saved me in the end was the realization that the voice that asked 'Would you like to die today?' was more *me* than the voice that answered. It was a detached and objective me that asked the question, and it was my depression that answered.

It cannot be said too strongly that a depressed person and his or her depression are separate. You are not your depression. Dr Rush lists the signs and symptoms which constitute depression. Read them and you will see exactly what depression is: a condition that affects you but is not intrinsically you.

That may sound like picking at words, but actually there is a considerable difference. Define the condition, and in some way you have put a net round it. Simply doing that can help you to control it.

There are of course many many different cures for depression. Pills, vitamins, hormones, psychotherapy, psychoanalysis, hypnosis, electric shocks, religion . . . even time. I constantly get letters from people claiming that such and such a remedy worked wonders for them. That does not mean it will work for everyone, but it does mean that it is worth keeping an open mind. If one remedy does not work, try another.

Dr Rush, having reviewed various treatments, from ECT to antidepressants, puts his faith in cognitive therapy. This is a relatively new approach to depression and a successful one, and represents a reaction away from psychoanalysis, which is expensive and long drawn out – even if a patient gets better, does analysis or time effect the cure? Cognitive therapy aims to get you 'roadworthy' quicker. It offers a perfectly comprehensible set of techniques designed to help you unlearn negative ways of thinking and build confidence. It offers what most depressed people want most: immediate help and the sense that they are helping themselves.

Many depressions, it seems, arise from chemical changes in the body. But what gives rise to those changes? For one person it might be the death of a parent; for another a display of meanness or bad temper. It is not that the second person is more inadequate than the first, merely that moving into depressive gear because someone you love is in a bad mood is unrealistic.

So often depressive moods are sparked off by trivialities, or rather by our negative reactions to trivialities. To ask someone to *stop* thinking negatively is not helpful. To analyse exactly *why* they are thinking negatively is time-consuming. But trying to *change the route* of their thinking is helpful; before a train of thought turns into the well-worn ruts of despair it is sidetracked along a more positive set of rails. 'My husband was surly, which means he hates me, which means I might as well kill myself' can be re-routed into 'My husband was surly, which means he was probably feeling low, which means I can probably do something to cheer him up.'

I remember, under analysis, wondering what good it would do me to find out the root cause of my depression. Thinking back, there were many reasons for my recovering, analysis certainly being one. But at the time cognitive therapy would have been an attractive proposition. We all know how simple techniques like yoga and relaxation can have a beneficial effect on the mind. Equally simple techniques of the mind can beneficially affect the body.

Virginia Ironside

Author's Preface

Today, depression is considered a major public health problem; a problem not only because the incidence of depression is relatively high—surveys suggest that as many as 15 per cent of adults have some depressive symptoms at any given time—but also because most cases of depression go unrecognized and untreated.

Depression can disrupt basic biological drives such as hunger, sex and sleep, and it can virtually extinguish our social instincts. Whenever we are depressed, we become seclusive, lose interest in other people, our self-esteem plummets and life ceases to offer enjoyment or pleasure. We even behave in ways that exacerbate rather than relieve our suffering. Depression contributes to a variety of social problems that range from breakdown in personal relationships, and academic or occupational failure, to alcoholism, drug addiction and juvenile delinquency. The most tragic outcome, of course, is suicide. More than 30 000 suicides are reported each year in the United States, and the real number may be three to four times higher—suicide attempts number in the hundreds of thousands.

With this sort of track record, it seems important to me that more people should realize that depressions are treatable disorders, be able to identify them when they occur, and be put in the picture with regard to our present knowledge about the causes and treatments.

Most of us use the word 'depression' quite legitimately to describe a mixture of feelings such as sadness, frustration and disappointment. So it may be confusing to find that doctors and psychiatrists use the word in rather a different way. To them, depression is a syndrome—that is, a specific set of signs and symptoms, and these involve more than just subjective reports of feelings. Moreover, because modern research has revealed that there are different kinds of depression that arise from different causes and respond to different treatments, the phrases 'depressive disorders' or 'affective disorders' are often used in preference to the blanket term 'depression'.

Most people are familiar with depression in one or another of its forms. Because it is likely to strike a common chord, I felt that starting this book with an account of the depression I experienced would be a helpful way into the subject. As theories of depression throughout the ages and the occurrence of depression among people worldwide are interesting facets of the subject, I then include a short history of depression and a section on its prevalence across cultures. The main body of the book takes a look at the way depressions are diagnosed, the various kinds of depression, their causes so far as we can ascertain, and the different treatments that have been developed to combat this perplexing set of disorders.

I wished to avoid burdening the text with long expositions of research studies and peppering it with references to scientific works. So I have outlined important relevant studies and, where necessary, gone into the biology of certain reactions. This does not assume any knowledge of the subject on the part of the reader; I believe it is perfectly possible to explain complex reactions without being too technical or, for that matter, too simplistic. Anyone interested in following up certain aspects will find my sources listed at the back of the book.

Much of the information we have about depression has been accumulated over the last 30 years, and continues apace. No doubt half of the data given credence today will require substantial revision in the next five years. So the statements and views I put forward in this volume are really a snapshot of a rapidly growing body of knowledge about depression. We do not have all the answers yet, and certainly the relationship between the biological and psychological factors that we think precipitate or maintain depression remains controversial. Even so, depressions are among the most treatable of all psychiatric disorders. With 'new breakthroughs' as always just around the corner, I am sure we can anticipate an even better understanding of depression, and the corollaries to that will be more effective treatment and better methods of prevention.

A. John Rush M.D.
Dallas, Texas

1

The experience of depression

For I am weary, and am overwrought
With too much toil, with too much care
distraught,
And with the iron crown of anguish crowned.

HENRY WADSWORTH LONGFELLOW (1807–1882)

From time to time, virtually every one of us confronts an event to which we respond with feelings of despondency, frustration or sadness. We may feel incapable of mustering sufficient energy to solve the problem with our usual skills. By contrast, similar frustrations or disappointments may encourage other people to become more introspective and think of alternatives to the situations confronting them.

While frustration and disappointment may be accompanied by a mood of sadness or despondency, they do not necessarily end in an illness that requires medical or psychiatric intervention. During times of frustration, indecision, sadness and concern—what most people would refer to as 'depression'—we may have trouble falling or staying asleep, we feel less energetic and may tend to eat too much or perhaps lose our appetite. Mostly these episodes are self-limiting and do not require professional intervention.

A first-hand account

Just after I accepted the assignment to write this book, an unusual series of circumstances provided me with an unwelcome opportunity to experience depression at first hand.

It was in the summer that I first noticed I had trouble reading papers and notes, particularly after coming indoors from the bright Texas sunshine. At first I tended to ignore my blurred vision, attributing it to light sensitivity. But it remained clouded.

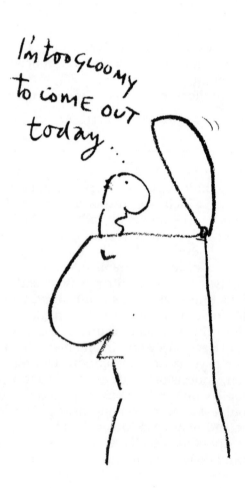

A month later, while sitting in a local cinema, I placed my hand over my right eye and noticed that the cloudiness went away. When I covered my left eye and looked out of my right, however, I was shocked to find that I was unable to see the left-hand side of the screen. Something was definitely wrong. I immediately recalled my neurology lessons. The cause of this visual loss was either in my eye or in the part of my brain that controls vision. Was it a brain tumour, an eye tumour, a stroke, or what? Anxiety, fear and dread prevailed. Perhaps if I ignored it, it would get better. What should I do?

The following day I saw a neurologist, who examined me carefully. It was not my brain; it was something in my eye. I was quite relieved that the possibility of a brain tumour had been ruled out.

The next visit was to my ophthalmist. 'Everything looks fine, except that there is something pushing your retina out.' (The retina is the inside covering of the eye.) That 'something', of course, could have been either a tumour or a tear in the retina.

Another specialist was called in, a retinologist this time. He would make the final diagnosis. After several tests, he announced sternly that I needed emergency eye surgery because my retina was torn. I was euphoric. With a giant smile, I agreed to have the operation. The doctor was bewildered at such a positive response—most patients do not look forward to eye surgery with such enthusiasm—until he realized that his diagnosis had removed my fears of an eye tumour.

During the entire diagnostic process, which took three days, fear and concern about my *life* were uppermost in my mind. Once we had settled on the need for emergency surgery to repair a retinal tear, my thoughts turned to concern about my *vision*. By this time, the sight in my right eye had become even worse. It began to dawn on me that, if the defect were not corrected, I would in essence be blind, because my left eye has been weak since birth. On its own, the left eye was unable to focus well enough for me to

19

decipher a single word. If surgery on the right eye failed, I would be unable to read or drive a car—in fact I would be totally incapable of carrying on with my job of teaching, writing and seeing patients.

A host of worries plagued me. What sort of work, if any, would I be able to do? Was I insured against disability? After many years of study and postgraduate training, was I to lose everything I had worked for? What had I done to deserve this? Why me? I was told that about 95 per cent of retinal tear repairs were successful, but this did not convince me that I would not be one of the unlucky ones.

The night before surgery, several close friends visited me. Their presence reassured me that, even if I did become blind, there would be people around who cared. They helped to take my mind off disasters that had not happened. As I drifted off to sleep, memories of the complicated surgical procedures I had seen as a medical student flashed through my mind. My faith in modern medicine was high, but it was tempered by the thought that surgeons are only human.

The operation was neither particularly unpleasant nor terribly painful. The surgeon reported that the operation had gone well. I was to stay in bed for a few weeks.

I had not anticipated that I would be immobile for several weeks, with a patch over my one good eye! This regimen, clearly excellent for my retina, was no therapy for my spirits. I was subjected to one of the most acutely frustrating situations I have ever encountered. Whereas previously I had been an avid reader of newspapers and all sorts of books and journals, now I couldn't even read my mail, let alone write a cheque to help sort out my affairs. The television was a blur and I had to shave by feel. I was helpless and totally dependent on other people.

The days became endless. I started to feel dissatisfied with just about everything, and only visits from friends and relatives provided transient relief. What if my sight did not return? How could I continue to lecture if I couldn't do all the reading and preparation needed? What would the rest of my life be like if I was blind? My broody pessimism was a typical reaction.

Social visits from friends became highly significant events during the day, but even these I viewed with mixed feelings. On the one hand, their presence was a relief and a distraction, and I appreciated their assistance and attention. Then again, the visits served as a reminder of the dependent situation I found myself in. Was I to live like this for ever?

While at times I felt like giving up, certain thoughts reassured me. I repeatedly reminded myself that uncertainty about my recovery would not last for ever. Sooner or later, I would know for sure whether or not my sight would return. Even if the news was bad, I promised myself I would cope somehow.

After three weeks, the bandages were removed and several more weeks of impaired vision followed, but after that my sight returned in full. I got back to work enthusiastically, appreciating more deeply the value of health, particularly sight. Now I was much more conscious of my vulnerability to injury. At the age of 37, I became aware that my body, to which I had paid little attention over the years, could suddenly and without notice disrupt or threaten life as I knew it.

Thoughts and feelings

Now let us examine my experience more closely. The table on page 22 summarizes the events involved, and my related thoughts and feelings. Notice that particular events led to specific thoughts, which in turn partly determined my mood. Hence, when the neurologist declared that the problem was a defect in my eye, I was *relieved* that it was not a brain disease.

On the other hand, a single event often gave rise to conflicting thoughts and feelings. My friends' visits provided some relief, yet because I could see no end to my state of helplessness, they also increased my sense of shame and dread. Thus the feelings we experience are greatly influenced by the thoughts we have. Those thoughts are coloured by our previous life experiences and by our current emotional state.

The pattern of events and related thoughts and feelings

Events	Thoughts	Feelings
Unable to see after coming in from sunshine.	Must be light-sensitive; ignore it.	Neutral
Unable to see in cinema.	There's something wrong with my vision. Maybe I have a brain tumour or some other disease. What should I do?	Fear, panic
Neurologist says it's not in my brain.	It's not a brain disease, anyway!	Relief
	What's wrong with my eye?	New fear
Ophthalmist says there's something pushing my retina out.	It's a tumour!	More fear
Retinologist says I need surgery for a torn retina.	Thank goodness, it's not an eye tumour. What is surgery like?	Relief More fear
Waiting for surgery.	What if my vision doesn't return? I'll be out of work and have nothing left.	Fear
Three weeks of rest in bed.	It will be horrible to be blind. Let's hope for the best.	Depression and boredom

(continues opposite)

Events	Thoughts	Feelings
Friends' visits during rehabilitation.	It's great to know friends care.	Relief
	I can't do anything or care for myself.	Shame, depression and helplessness

If we study my thoughts and consider their actual structure and content, it is striking that many were statements or conclusions, snap judgements that represented only one possibility at a given time. Later, these judgements proved to be false. For instance, my conclusion, 'I must be light-sensitive', was simply untrue. The supposition, 'It's a tumour', was also false. I did consider more optimistic possibilities, such as a torn retina, but fear made me less willing to believe them.

The benefit of experience

Our past experiences influence our responses to current events. So, if we lose or risk losing something, be it a physical ability, a valued article, even an opportunity, that thing usually becomes more desirable or important to us. My temporary loss of vision was no exception. When the depression lifted and my sight was fully restored, driving my car was as thrilling as when I first passed my test.

The threat of a serious medical illness that could have led to disability or death also made me sensitive in another way. For example, a few weeks after returning to work, Arthur, a young man of 29, came to see me for treatment of his depression. He had been referred to me by his radiotherapist, who was treating him for metastatic cancer of the kidney. It appeared likely that he would die within four to six months.

In the first interview, I was unusually distracted and nervous, for Arthur's situation was a poignant reminder of my own vulnerability to illness and death. My own worries interfered with my ability to give him my undivided attention. As the sessions continued, I was better able to focus my attention and much less nervous. After about eight weeks (during which time his depression lifted), we discussed the first session in detail. To my surprise, he told me that it had been the most important interaction he had ever had; he had felt that I could really understand what he was going through.

He concluded his treatment by saying there were many things that could happen that were worse than cancer. He was referring to depression. You might think this sounds shocking. But just consider the person who suffers a severe depression that persists for months and months. For him, life ceases to have all meaning. By contrast, people with the severest physical illness may still find value and pleasure in at least some aspects of their lives.

Before the operation I would, of course, have been concerned about Arthur and I would have tried to help him. But as a result of having experienced my operation and its attendant anxieties, his situation reactivated worries about my own life—worries which initially seemed to interfere with my professional competence, but which seemed to allow a deeper understanding of his dilemma.

Situational versus clinical depression

I had experienced what is called 'situational' depression, sometimes called 'reactive' depression, and it is different from a passing mood of sadness. Nobody is immune to situational depression, and virtually

everyone will experience one or more episodes during a lifetime. In such cases a specific event, or series of events, leads to a sustained mood of sadness often mixed with anxiety. Although sadness and helplessness may be felt quite acutely, a situational depression is self-limited—that is, it usually only lasts days or a few weeks and will be alleviated if whatever caused it in the first place is set to rights. Help from a doctor or psychiatrist is often unnecessary, and this sort of depression does not predispose you to more severe forms of depression.

The severer sorts of depression very often require treatment, and so are called 'clinical' depressions. Details of these (namely bipolar and unipolar illness, secondary and endogenous depression) are given in Chapter 5.

In a few people, what starts off as a situational

depression can deteriorate into a clinical one. The sad mood, negative outlook, impaired concentration and reduced self-esteem may begin to interfere with problem-solving and coping in everyday life. Difficulties at work, problems with close personal relationships and trouble with all forms of social interaction may arise as a result. As the depressed person recognizes that the problems are beginning to multiply, he or she may initially struggle to cope. But the depression will already have sapped energy, interfered with sleep and otherwise reduced the capacity to cope. A sense of failure, demoralization, helplessness and deeper depression may ensue.

What is the difference?

How do we distinguish a situational depression from a clinical one? Let me return to my own case for a moment. My depression lasted a matter of weeks. I certainly experienced a change in mood. Sadness and fears were present. My energy level dropped, my view of the future became more pessimistic and uncertain. But this was clearly a response to a distressing and potentially dangerous situation. As soon as the situation clarified and resolved itself, my feelings of fear and sadness began to disappear. Note too, that during the depression, my mood lifted when friends visited me or when good things happened. I could still enjoy music, for instance. I continued to think about how I would cope, whatever the consequences of the surgery. Of course, I desperately hoped that I would not lose my sight, but I assumed that I would carry on somehow if I did. These then are the hallmarks of situational depression.

Clinical depression lasts much longer than a few weeks; it is often present for many months before a person seeks treatment. The mood in situational depression is closely tied to the situation itself. If the situation changes for the better, so does the mood. In clinical depression, the mood may be independent of any situation. If circumstances improve, only partial relief of the mood ensues. Sadness, anxiety and worry in situational depression do not stop a person from making the best of things and dealing with interim problems. Clinically depressed people usually see no alternative to their feelings of helplessness and hopelessness.

Someone suffering from situational depression can be reassured by friends and relations who rally round. Clinically depressed people often dismiss reassurance and signs of kindness as false gestures of concern. They may cease to take pleasure in the things they previously found enjoyable. Finally, unlike situational depression, clinical depression is associated with profound disturbances in bodily functions (sleep, appetite, sexual interest).

We have learned that in Western society too many depressions, perhaps the majority, go unrecognized, undiagnosed and untreated. Unfortunately, an unwarranted sense of shame has been attached to so-called 'mental' illness. The erroneous belief that it is a sign of personal or moral weakness often prevents people from seeking help.

2

Sadness, madness and melancholia

Man's inhumanity to man
Makes countless thousands mourn.

ROBERT BURNS (1756–1796)

Ancient and Biblical writings provide the earliest accounts of depression. The earliest suicide note we have was written well over three thousand years ago by an Egyptian seer in the reign of the pharaoh Akhnaton. On the whole, the Ancients believed that suicide and suicidal thoughts were a specific form of behaviour resulting from stresses such as imprisonment, and loss of status or fortune, rather than a symptom of a more all-embracing mental condition.

Mental illness was as prevalent among the Jews of the Scriptures as it was among the Egyptians. In the Old Testament, Hannah, mother of the prophet Samuel, apparently suffered from severe neurosis. King Saul had recurrent depressions and was prone to both suicidal and homicidal impulses. Generally, mental illness was considered to be God's curse for disobedience. Even in modern times, this view has provided the rationale for persecuting, and even executing, perfectly innocent but mentally unbalanced people.

The Greeks and Romans

Greek writings provide the earliest well-documented accounts of particular disorders of the mind. The early Greeks tended to liken mental illness with the actions of gods. For instance, Ajax, a doughty hero of the *Iliad*, was said to have been temporarily robbed of his mental faculties by the gods.

Hippocrates (460–377 BC) was among the first to recognize that disorders of the mind originated from natural causes, and were not visited on people at the whim of the gods. Even today, the language of psychiatry is couched in terminology developed by Hippocrates. For example, the words 'melancholy', 'melancholia', come from the ancient Greek for 'black bile'—a bodily fluid, or 'humour', thought to create feelings of sadness and depression in human beings. One of Hippocrates' own case histories accurately describes the symptoms:

> 'In Thesus, a woman of melancholic turn of mind from some accidental cause of sorrow, while still going about, became affected with loss of sleep, aversion of food and had thirst and nausea . . . On the first . . . night, frights, much talking, despondency, slight fever; in the morning, frequent spasms, and when they ceased, she was incoherent and talked obscurely, pains frequently, great and continued. On the second in the same state; had no sleep, fever more acute. On the third, the spasms left her, but coma, and . . . again awakened, started up and could not contain herself . . .'

Hippocrates underlined the basic importance of the brain in the development of mental disorders. For melancholia, he prescribed abstinence from all excesses, sexual abstinence, a vegetable diet, exercise short of fatigue and bleeding if needed. He also apparently subscribed to an idea put forward later by the philosopher Theophrastus (372–287 BC), that black bile, a toxic product of digestion, might account for melancholia. This belief probably constitutes the first 'biological' theory of the cause of depression.

Although in some respects Hippocrates' work survives to this day, many of the benefits of his enlightened approach to mental illness, including his attempts to separate psychology from mystical prejudice and to view the human body and mind as a single unit, were lost after his death.

The recommendations of the Roman physician and medical writer Celsus, in the first century AD, rate as some of the earliest psychotherapeutic treatments for depression, and are not far removed from some of today's psychotherapeutic procedures (Chapter 9):

'The belly is to be kept as soft as possible; terrors are to be dispersed, and rather good hopes are to be given. Entertainment must be sought in amusing stories and diversions, such as the person in health used to be most pleased with. If there are any works of his performing, they must be commended and placed before his eyes. His groundless sorrow is to be mildly reprimanded. Arguments must be offered now and then to persuade him that in those very things which disturb him there is more matter for joy than anxiety . . .'

Another physician, Aretaeus of Cappadocia (AD 30–90), was the first to distinguish different types of depression. He recognized organic depression (now called endogenous) and external depression (now called situational) as two separate illnesses. He also identified manic as opposed to depressive episodes (see Chapter 5), and in doing so seems to have realized that some depressive illnesses include only recurrent bouts of depression (what we now call unipolar illness), whereas others include episodes of mania and depression (now called bipolar illness). He emphasized as causes 'anger and grief and sad dejection of mind', in contrast to his predecessors' emphasis on black bile.

The Greek physician Galen (AD 130–200) stands out above all other medics of his time on account of his encyclopedic works on medical matters. Though few of his descriptions of mental disorders are close to modern descriptions, like Hippocrates he viewed the

individual as an integral, psychobiological unit. He believed that psychological functions were centred in the brain, and that it was the brain that was directly affected in melancholia.

The Dark and Middle Ages

After Galen, Western civilization appears to have reverted to the belief that possession and supernatural forces were the causes of mental illness. St Augustine of Hippo (AD 354–430), a Christian theologian and philosopher and influential personality in the Western Church of his time, wrote: 'There are no diseases that do not arise from witchery and hence from the mind.' This attitude unquestionably contributed to the later inhumane treatment of witches, many of whom were very probably mentally disturbed.

While many Westerners believe that science and medicine spread from the West to the East, the reverse is actually the case. The Near East, Egypt and Mesopotamia were responsible for much of the early scientific thought on which Greek learning and, later, Western science were based.

Throughout the Muslim Empire, during the Dark and Middle Ages, medicine continued the traditions inherited from Greek medicine, so that mental illness was ascribed more to natural causes than to supernatural forces. One of the most influential philosopher-scientists of Islam was the Persian Avicenna (AD 980–1037), also nicknamed Prince of Physicians. He did not recognize the influence of demons as a causal agent in mental illness. While he believed that the seat of melancholia was to be found in the stomach, liver and spleen, he also ascribed mental illness to disorders of the brain. He introduced an eclectic psychology, that is, he also discussed the role of thought and emotion in such disturbances.

Jewish medicine also made significant advances in the Middle Ages. The distinguished Rabbi Moses ben Maimon, or Maimonides (AD 1135–1204), a celebrated philosopher and physician, acknowledged a close relationship between mental and physical health and moral principles.

The Renaissance

Renaissance thinkers, influenced by the philosophical, medical and mathematical texts of antiquity, turned back to nature, to observation and to experimentation. For example, the Swiss physician Paracelsus (AD 1493–1541)—his real name was Philippus Theophrastus Bombastus von Hohenheim—attributed natural causes to *all* physical and mental illness, and in his *Diseases That Deprive Man of His Reason*, he implied that the unconscious played a role in hysteria.

Johann Weyer (1515–1588) was a Belgian doctor who was prominent amongst those who viewed witchcraft as mere superstition and believed that witches were psychotic rather than 'possessed'. His clinical methods formed the basis for the first proper diagnostic system of psychiatric disorders, formulated by Emil Kraepelin in the nineteenth century.

Timothy Bright, a resident physician at London's St Bartholomew's Hospital, was the first to recognize suicide as a manifestation of despair. His *Treatise on Melancholia* (1586) was the first psychiatric monograph in English to describe the feelings of melancholic patients in precise detail.

Robert Burton, a scholar, writer and Anglican clergyman, wrote *The Anatomy of Melancholy* (in 1621). In this work, he summarized the existing theories of depression and helped pave the way for subsequent scientific recognition of the depressive disorders. He depicted a wide range of depression, from natural grief over death or separation to various forms of clinical depression, including chronic recurrent depressions. He lists the complaints of melancholics as follows:

'One complains of want, a second of servitude, another of a secret or incurable disease; of some deformity of body, of some loss, danger, death of friend, shipwreck, persecution, imprisonment, disgrace, repulse . . .'

However perspicacious we may think these descriptions are, and however sympathetic the approach of people like Johann Weyer, not all Renaissance thought was so enlightened. King James I (1603–1625) was a firm believer in demonology, and assumed that any deranged person was bewitched.

Not until the eighteenth century did the situation for the mentally ill begin to improve. In general, disturbed people were left at large in the community as long as they caused no public disturbance. They were usually looked after by friends and relatives, but several general hospitals in Paris, Hamburg, Erfurt and London—among others—began to accommodate mentally disturbed patients in the late eighteenth century.

The Enlightenment

The hospitals of the Middle Ages were primarily ecclesiastical institutions unrelated to medical care. By the sixteenth century, these institutions began to serve social rather than religious or medical goals, a role that lasted until the nineteenth century. For example, the priory of Bethlehem in Bishopsgate, London, later became a lunatic asylum (Bedlam), notorious for its treatment of mentally disturbed people as spectacles for derision and entertainment.

The American and the French Revolutions confirmed a growing concern about individual liberty. Against this historical backdrop, the French physician Phillippe Pinel (1745–1826) began a programme of asylum reform and humane treatment of the insane for which he is distinguished in the history of modern psychiatry. As director of the mental institutions of Le Bicêtre and La Salpêtrière in Paris, he took the revolutionary step of removing the chains from some of the inmates on an experimental basis. He did away with some of the more barbaric treatments such as bleeding, purging and blistering, in favour of therapy that included friendly contact and discussion with his patients.

At about the same time, an English philanthropist, William Tuke (1732–1822), who was a Quaker, and a tea and coffee merchant by trade, founded the York Retreat. This was an institute for the insane where humane treatment of the inmates was the order of the day. Tuke emphasized that patients should be treated as rational human beings and should be encouraged to display self-control. The enlightened views of Pinel and Tuke were influential. In Belgium, Joseph Guislain (1797–1860) unchained patients and advocated humane treatment in hospitals in Ghent. He was known as the liberator of the insane. In America, Benjamin Rush (1745–1813), who is known as the 'father of American psychiatry', adopted a progressive approach and advocated the need to combine psychological treatment with physical remedies.

The beginning of the nineteenth century saw an even greater focus on descriptive diagnosis and clinical observation. Jean Esquirol (1722–1840), a student of Pinel, made important innovations in the treatment of the mentally ill. He differentiated between hallucinations (disorders of sensation and perception) and delusions (fixed false beliefs). He also emphasized the importance of environment and age as precipitating factors in mental illness. Another of Pinel's students, Jean Pierre Falret (1794–1870), studied suicidal tendencies and also turned his attention to the relationship between mania and depression.

A new understanding

Eighteenth-century interest in mental illness had been marked by the recognition of certain different mental disorders and a tendency towards humane and enlightened treatment. These trends were crystallized by nineteenth- and early twentieth-century study, which led to an orderly system of classifying mental illness based on descriptive diagnosis.

One eminent Victorian doctor was Henry Maudsley (1835–1918), founder of the famous London psychiatric teaching hospital which bears his name. Maudsley espoused Darwin's theory of evolution, and interpreted mental illness as a failure of adaptation; as evidence of discord between man and his environment. Thus, someone who was mentally ill could neither bend circumstances to suit himself, nor could he accommodate himself to circumstances. In his texts *The Physiology of Mind* (1876) and *The Pathology of Mind* (1879), Maudsley outlined the influence of the society in which we live on the symptoms of depression and melancholia.

On the Continent, diagnostic advances were being made. Emil Kraepelin (1856–1926), an influential German psychiatrist, established a system for diagnosing specific disorders. He clearly distinguished between two important complexes of mental illness:

between 'manic-depressive insanity', an episodic, non-deteriorating disorder, and 'dementia praecox', later called 'schizophrenia', a more progressive deteriorating condition. The term 'schizophrenia' was in fact first advanced by Eugen Bleuler (1857–1939), a Swiss psychiatrist who introduced greater exactitude in the naming of mental illnesses.

Adolf Meyer (1866–1950), a Swiss-born neurologist and a powerful influence on American psychiatry, believed that current stresses on an individual and his or her developmental history were important causes of mental illness. Meyer and his contemporaries, including of course Sigmund Freud (1856–1939), emphasized the social and cultural factors underlying mental illness.

Although other psychologists had laid stress on the unconscious, it was Sigmund Freud who explicitly postulated that all irrational behaviour could be explained by unconscious motives. To deal with mental disorders, he developed a therapy called psychoanalysis.

The works of Freud, Karl Abraham (1877–1925) and Sandor Rado (1890–1972) are the cornerstones of psychoanalytic thinking about depression. In *Mourning and Melancholia* (1917), Freud described melancholia as a period of self-torment during which the emotional representation of the lost person is punished until it is sufficiently devalued and the wounds are thereby healed. Karl Abraham stressed the role of ambivalence or mutually opposed feelings in the development of depression. He hypothesized that, when a loved one is lost, the mourner is left with mixed or ambivalent feelings. Negative feelings previously directed at the departed person no longer have an object, so instead are directed at the self. Thus depression represents anger turned on the self.

Early in his career, Sandor Rado also wrote of how depressions were ill-fated attempts to adapt to losses. Later, however, he began to question this formulation.

Edward Bibring, another of the psychoanalytic school, believed that failure to achieve a desired goal or the love of a person produced a loss of self-esteem and subsequent depression. (Loss of self-esteem was seen as a common denominator in all depressive conditions.) Therefore he proposed that depression could result from situations other than just the loss of a loved one by separation or death.

Although it was realized, particularly by Rado, that not all depressions could be explained as anger turned inward or a loss of self-esteem, and that various mechanisms might be involved, early psychoanalytic theories did not recognize different types of depression.

New treatments

The hallmark of psychiatric treatment at the turn of the twentieth century was psychoanalysis. This simply concentrated on giving the patient insight into his or her own motives and conflicts, and did not involve any physical treatment. Of course, physical treatments had long been held to alleviate or cure mental illness, witness the early penchant for purging and bleeding. Later, in the nineteenth century, ducking in icy water, whirling patients around at high speed in mechanical devices and even infecting them with diseases such as malaria and smallpox were believed to be beneficial.

However, in the 1930s a Hungarian psychiatrist introduced what can be regarded as the first specific biological treatment for severe mental disorders. It was widely believed that convulsions helped schizophrenics, and in Budapest in 1934 Ladislas Meduna started to treat schizophrenics using camphor as an inhalant to induce seizures.

ECT and antidepressants

Then in 1938, Ugo Cerletti and Lucio Bini, two Italian psychiatrists, induced convulsions by passing an electric current through the brain by means of electrodes placed on the forehead. Following their lead, Lothar Kalinowski introduced electroconvulsive therapy, ECT as it was called, in the United States. The advent of ECT constituted a major advance in the treatment of severe mental disorders. Subsequent research has shown that ECT is only mildly effective in treating schizophrenia, but that it is very effective in treating severe depressions.

Another significant step forward in the biological treatment of depression was made in the 1950s, with the discovery of specific antidepressant medications. It was noticed that isoniazid, a drug used to treat people with tuberculosis, induced elevation of mood. Reserpine, on the other hand, a drug used to control hypertension or high blood pressure, was found to produce depression in about 15 per cent of people treated with it.

These discoveries led to a host of investigations designed to identify the underlying neurophysiology and chemistry of depression. As a result, it was found that reserpine reduced the activity of neurotransmitters (the chemical substances that help nerve cells to communicate with each other). By contrast, isoniazid made more of these neurotransmitters available. These findings gave rise to the idea that specific chemical changes in the brain could lead to depression (the first chemical theory of depression). Shortly afterwards the first antidepressant medications, similar to isoniazid, were discovered. They were called monoamine oxidase inhibitors, or MAOIs, after the enzyme monoamine oxidase, which they inhibit.

Further advances came in 1957 with the discovery of 'tricyclic' antidepressants (so called because of their three-ring molecular structure). R. Kuhn, a Swiss psychiatrist, astutely recognized the antidepressant effects of these drugs when they were being tested as treatments for schizophrenia. Subsequently, in literally hundreds of careful studies, the tricyclic antidepressants have been shown to be powerfully effective in the treatment of various depressive disorders.

In 1949, John Cade, an Australian psychiatrist, found that the element lithium was effective in treating mania, This was extensively tested in carefully designed research studies by Mogens Schou, a Danish doctor, and others in the 1960s and 1970s. Its introduction has radically altered the psychiatric approach to the treatment of manic-depressive or bipolar illness. It has reduced the use of ECT in treating mania, and has undoubtedly saved thousands of patients from the prolonged hospitalization that this debilitating disorder previously required.

A new class of antidepressant called tetracyclics (because of their four-ring chemical structure) was developed in the 1970s. The success of drug therapy to date has stimulated much research into the biological basis of behaviour and emotional states.

The last decade has also witnessed the development of short-term psychotherapies that have been specially designed for the treatment of depression (see Chapter 9). It seems these newer psychotherapies may help in the treatment of some depressions that respond poorly to the medications currently available.

Treatments for people with depression have substantially improved as specific medications and psychotherapies have been developed. As we come to understand the psychological and biochemical bases of depression better, it is hoped that we will be able to develop preventive techniques.

3

How common is depression?

To eat bread without hope is still slowly to
starve to death.

PEARL S. BUCK (b. 1892)

A major difficulty in studying the prevalence and
incidence of depression round the world has been that
of diagnosis. Depression in the United States or
Europe may not look like depression in India, Iran or
Kenya. As Henry Maudsley noted, the content of
specific delusions in depression may be affected by the
cultural context.

It is striking to note that the term 'depression' is
missing from the vocabulary of a number of non-
Western cultures. This does not mean that depression
as defined in the West does not exist. Rather, it may be
experienced and conceptualized differently.

Is depression more common in one culture than
another? The first table here shows the percentage of
people receiving treatment from depression through
various institutions and clinical services in a number
of countries. These figures combine all different types
of depression. But we should interpret them with
caution. Deciding when a person is depressed is no
easy matter. The tendency to diagnose depression will

41

People actually treated for depression

Country	Percentage of population	Year
Guyana (formerly British Guiana)	7·0	1956
Canada (French)	4·7	1970
(English)	6·0	1970
(Indians)	3·0–4·8	1970
(Eskimos)	12·0	1970
Czechoslovakia	12·3	1967
Egypt	13·2	1968
England	16·6	1969
Hongkong	7·0	1972
India	4·9	1964
Israel	3·7	1960
Italy	13·0	1964
Japan	7·1	1964
Kenya (blacks)	1·5	1953
(whites)	22·0	1953
People's Republic of China	5·0	1974
Philippines	13·1	1972
USA (whites)	12·9	1972

differ widely from culture to culture. Even amongst those people who do seek treatment, there are large differences in the frequency with which depression is diagnosed. Moreover, it is difficult to count the actual number of people who are depressed in each country. The figures refer only to those who did seek treatment. Depressed people in one culture may tend not to seek treatment, whereas in another they may be more likely to see themselves as needing treatment. All that can be said of these percentages, then, is that they show that no culture is immune to depression and that it is not simply a disorder of Western civilization.

Other studies have shown that two to three times as many women as men appear to be depressed at any given time. This ratio holds across different cultures and it is not, as far as we know, affected by the degree to which women are liberated.

The next table shows a series of figures that may more accurately reflect the true prevalence of depression (the total number of people suffering at any given time). These figures were arrived at by surveying samples of the population at large, regardless of whether they had been under treatment at any time.

People estimated to be suffering from depression

Country	Prevalence (cases per 1 000 population)	Year
Czechoslovakia	1·5	1964
Denmark	7·8	1961
India (countrywide)	2·7	1964
(urban)	6·9	1967
(rural)	1·5	1972
Ireland	10·4	1961
Japan	0·2	1963
Korea	0·3	1961
Sweden	0·2	1953
Taiwan	0·7	1953
Uganda	0·9	1973
Australia (Aborigines)	1 case per 2 360	1973

Again, the figures cover a very wide range. In general, the rates in non-Western countries are much lower than in Western Europe or the United States, but we do not know whether sociocultural, genetic, dietary, religious or other factors might account for these differences.

How culture affects depression

Does a depressed person in India appear the same, behave in the same way and experience the same symptoms as a depressed person in the United States? In Africa, depressed persons rarely experience self-blame, guilt or suicidal rumination as part of their depression, whereas Western depressions typically involve much guilt and self-blame, and predispose to suicide. Arabs who develop depression tend to complain of difficulties in digestion, abdominal pain, and loss of appetite and weight. Again, guilt, self-blame and suicide are rare. On the other hand, westernized and more affluent Arabs develop a depression more similar to that seen in the West.

The Senegalese, when depressed, do not appear deeply unhappy or miserable. Ideas of self-blame and guilt are absent; suicide is rare. Rather, depression is characterized by ideas of persecution (the person falsely believes that others are out to harm or take advantage of him or her), anxiety, disturbed sleep and appetite, and complaints of bodily aches and pains. In India, depression is likely to be associated with significant feelings of anxiety, an inner restlessness and physical aches and pains. Again, guilt feelings are rare.

In Indonesia, depression is characterized by a severe lack of energy and sleep disturbances. Feelings of sadness are often absent. Guilt feelings and feelings of inadequacy are rare. W. Pfeiffer, who has studied the subject, suggested that amongst depressed Indonesians feelings of inadequacy and guilt may be absent, because in Indonesia the worth of a person is not determined by what he or she achieves. Thus, although depression may reduce productivity and impair achievement, feelings of guilt do not follow. This might also explain why guilt and self-esteem are rare in other non-Western cultures which are less achievement-oriented.

Several studies have begun to identify what are

called culture-specific disorders that may be equivalent to depression. These disorders go by different names. They even appear rather different from what are usually classified as depressions. The Sioux and perhaps other Plains Indians in North America suffer from *tawatl ye snior*, meaning totally discouraged, which is characterized by feelings of helplessness, thoughts of death, and a preoccupation with ideas of ghosts and spirits. In Central and South America, *susto* or 'soul loss' is characterized by the sudden onset of weakness, loss of appetite, sleep difficulties, fear,

WHY?
Why did she
say that
I'm DEPRESSED?
Everyone knows that
I'm very cheerful.. If
I thought for a minute
that I was depressed..
I'd be very depressed..

Z
Z
Z
Z..

slowed-down behaviour (motor retardation), anxiety, sweating, diarrhoea and palpitations. These characteristics are similar to those seen in Western-type anxious or agitated depressions. The disorder can often be traced to a specific event and may result from breaking taboos or receiving a curse.

Socio-cultural theories of depression

What role do the traditions and practices of particular societies play in the development or expression of depression? A number of theories have been offered, but none has been accepted in preference to the others. For example, some people have viewed the extended family structure as a protective buffer against depression. Thus, early reports of the lower incidence of depression in non-Western cultures were explained by the predominant role of the extended family.

Another theory suggests that depression may be related to the level of social cohesion in a society. Social cohesion means how much members of the society share common values and expectations, and provide mutual support and assistance. There is some evidence to suggest that increased social cohesion is associated with a reduction in depression.

Other investigators have suggested that particular psychological mechanisms are fostered by the culture, and that these mechanisms may protect against depression. When people tend to blame others or the environment for their problems, rather than themselves, the chances of personal failure or incapacity leading to guilt and self-blame are reduced. A culture that sanctions low self-expectations and demands may protect individuals from frustration and reduce the frequency of perceived failure. In these cultures, relatively simple acts can maintain self-esteem or a positive view of the self.

One interesting theory proposed suggests that cultures which provide outlets for aggression will experience low levels of depression. A study that seems to support this view compared the rates of depression in Belfast, Northern Ireland, and a related, more peaceful community. In Belfast, during civil hostilities, depression rates decreased and the suicide rate dropped by more than 50 per cent. During these same hostilities, the rates of depression in the neighbouring community sharply increased.

In summary, then, we can say that there is no universal concept of depression. Many non-Western cultures do not have notions of depression equivalent to those held by Western mental health professionals. Yet in all cultures people suffer from depressive disorders similar to those found in the West, though they may be labelled differently, and regarded as having different causes and meanings.

On current evidence, it seems that depression is less common in non-Western cultures, or rather that symptoms such as guilt feelings, self-derogation and suicidal thinking (and suicide attempts) are less common.

4

Recognizing depression

Studies of emotion in different cultures suggest that there are seven primary emotions or feelings—sadness, joy, anger, fear, surprise, disgust and love. Each emotion is accompanied by unique facial expressions that help us to recognize the feeling in other people, even if they are from different cultural backgrounds. A sad person will tend to walk more slowly. The head droops, the eyes are downcast, and the shoulders are slumped as if he or she were carrying a heavy burden. There is a tendency to speak at the end of expiration, giving the voice a low and somewhat monotonous quality. A protruded lower lip, a down-turned mouth, a furrowed forehead, tearful-looking eyes, and a preoccupied appearance characterize the face of sadness. These then are the clues that we are all familiar with.

A psychiatrist, however, will use other criteria to identify or diagnose a depression. To the psychiatrist, depression is a syndrome, a special cluster of signs and symptoms recurrently seen in clinical practice. In this context, the words 'sign' and 'symptom' have specific meanings. *Signs* mean objective findings that can be observed by others, usually the diagnostician. *Symptoms* are those subjective complaints or states that can be identified and expressed by the patient.

Signs and symptoms of depression

The signs and symptoms that characterize depression are summarized in the table below.

Behaviour

Crying
Retardation or agitation
Social withdrawal or 'clinging' behaviour

Emotions

Sadness
Anger or irritability
Anxiety
Guilt
Mood swings on a daily basis

Thinking patterns

Helplessness—negative view of self
Hopelessness—negative view of the future
Worthlessness—self-blame, self-criticism
Indecisiveness
Difficulty in concentrating
Suicidal thinking
Hallucinations or delusions (psychotic depression)

(continues overleaf)

Bodily symptoms

Disordered sleep (insomnia or hypersomnia)
Appetite/weight changes (increase or decrease)
Decreased sexual interest/activity
Feeling weak, easily tired, lacking in energy
Menstrual irregularities
Changes in bowel habits (constipation/diarrhoea)
Aches and pains
Lack of interest in usually enjoyable activities or an inability
   to experience pleasure

The behavioural signs of depression are not difficult to
spot. However, one has to know a person fairly well
and over a period to notice an increasing reluctance
and distaste for social interaction, or a slowing down
of both thinking and actions, or alternatively a
speeding up. 'Clinging' behaviour is best described as
a desperate need to be with people, a need not to be
alone.

A feeling of intense sadness is typical of a
depressed person. However, sadness may not be the
only emotion experienced. Other mood changes may
involve increased feelings of anger and irritability,

fear, anxiety and tension or, at times, guilt and self-blame. Some depressions are characterized by a worsening of mood in the early morning when the person wakes up. This pattern is especially typical of melancholic depression (see page 54). Other types of depression may be associated with a worsening mood in the evening or at night. Still other depressions appear to involve a pervasive disturbance in mood that continues throughout the whole day.

Changes in thought and outlook

Changes in thinking patterns and outlook occur in most depressions. Depressed people often view themselves as helpless or unable to do anything about their situation. They are frequently extremely self-critical and self-blaming, and have a negative view of themselves. They may feel worthless, and even have delusions or preoccupations about what they believe are unforgivable past sins or irrevocable failures. Other changes in thinking pattern include a negative view of the future or a sense of hopelessness. For example, a depressed person who considers undertaking a particular task such as looking for a new job, may already anticipate failure and expect rejection by a prospective employer. These negative expectations therefore make him or her refrain from taking any action at all.

Such thought patterns can be very destructive. The individual feels more and more convinced, albeit wrongly, that he or she is worthless, helpless and defective and that the future holds no hope; suicide becomes a real consideration. Preoccupation with death and suicide characterize a large number of depressions and may lead to a suicide attempt if unchecked.

Furthermore, depressed people often find it difficult to make up their minds, even about simple matters. Even a decision such as what to buy for dinner becomes difficult. Part of the problem is that they have moderate or severe difficulty in concentrating or paying attention. This may be the result of obsessively negative thought, but in some depressions there is evidence that specific impairments in memory processes occur.

A person is said to be suffering from psychotic depression when he or she cannot readily distinguish between reality and fantasy, between the world that everyone else sees and hears and a private world of visual or auditory hallucinations. Typically, these hallucinations also have a sad or self-critical content. For example, people with a severe psychotic depression might report seeing a dead member of the family in the bedroom, or hear accusing voices blaming them for having caused the death of a loved one. In addition, they may develop fixed false beliefs or delusions involving the idea that something terrible or awful either has happened or will happen. They may believe, for example, that the world is coming to an end or that they have an incurable physical illness.

Bodily changes

Depression is also associated with a variety of bodily (somatic) symptoms. Most typically, there is a marked disturbance in sleeping patterns. Insomnia or difficulty in sleeping is common. The difficulty may be in falling asleep (early insomnia), staying asleep (middle insomnia), or waking up too early and being unable to get back to sleep (late insomnia). In some types of depression, there is apparent hypersomnia, a tendency to sleep too much.

A depressed person may also notice changes in appetite. In some cases, there may be a marked increase in the amount of food eaten and a consequent gain in weight. However, a noticeable decrease in appetite and weight loss is more usual.

Very often, depression is accompanied by a decrease in sexual activity and other normally pleasurable activities. In more severe cases, men may have erectile difficulties or be unable to climax. Women may become indifferent to their sexual partner or lose the ability to climax. During some depressions, they may also undergo changes in their menstrual cycle. Missed or irregular periods, and sometimes more frequent periods, are not uncommon.

If only my DOCTOR hadn't told me sleeplessness was a symptom of DEPRESSION - I'd never have known I had it...

calman

Victims of depression also complain that they feel weak, are easily tired and have much less energy than before.

Perhaps the commonest of symptoms is the inability to enjoy those things that previously gave pleasure. A satisfying job may suddenly seem pointless and boring. Hobbies can lose their appeal. Children become a millstone rather than a joy. In short, nothing feels worthwhile, meaningful or enjoyable.

Melancholic depression is a particular form of depression, characterized by a mood that does not respond to any positive or negative events within the environment. Severe weight loss, appetite loss, marked slowness in behaviour and thinking, early-morning worsening of mood and severe insomnia characterize this type of depression.

More than half of those suffering from depression will complain of specific aches and pains. Headaches are most common, although stomach-aches, back-aches, muscle-aches or joint pains are not rare. Some people may complain that they have difficulty breathing and feel as if they are suffocating. Palpitations or rapid heart-beats, diarrhoea, profuse sweating, and even episodes of panic that may last for several minutes to an hour are reported. During a bout of panic, a person becomes extremely anxious; several patients describing the experience to me have said they feel as if they were about to die. In his book, *Breakdown*, Stuart Sutherland, Professor of Experimental Psychology at Sussex University, who himself suffered a severe depression, described the feeling like this:

'The onset of my neurosis was marked by levels of physical anxiety that I would not have believed possible. If one is almost involved in a road accident, there is a delay of a second or two and then the pit of the stomach seems to fall out and one's legs go like jelly. It was this feeling multiplied a hundredfold that seized me at all hours of the day and night. My dreams were often pleasant, but as soon as I woke panic set in . . .'

At the beginning of a depression or during a mild depression, only a few of these symptoms will be present. Age, sex and cultural background also influence which signs and symptoms predominate, added to which not all depressions are alike. Particular symptoms are more likely to occur in conjunction with certain kinds of depression. So how then does the clinician diagnose depression?

Diagnosing depression

One recent advance in diagnostic methods has been the introduction of specific 'diagnostic criteria'. These are set out in the table shown on p. 56 and consist of specific signs and symptoms that clinicians have agreed constitute core elements typical of most people who suffer from a depression. They include unpredictable changes of mood, which usually involve feeling sad or 'blue', but at times may mean you feel angry, irritable, anxious or guilty. Additional criteria include a change in appetite and weight (an increase or decrease); changes in motor activity (agitation or sluggishness); sleep changes (either sleeping too much or too little); the presence of marked guilt or self-blame; suicidal thinking or action; difficulties in concentration and decision-making; a marked impairment in one's ability to enjoy the usually pleasurable aspects of life, and/or a decrease in sexual drive or interest. A distinct lack of energy, together with a tendency to become tired more quickly, are also often experienced. If a person suffers from altered moods and at least four of the remaining eight signs and symptoms enumerated above, and if these persist for longer than one week and cannot be attributed to grief, a diagnosis of depression can be made.

Components of a depressive episode

General change	Specific changes	Duration
	Four or more of the following:	
Awareness of mood swings beyond one's control	Change in appetite/weight	At least one week, and not attributable to grief
	Increased agitation/physical slowness (motor changes)	
	Changes in sleep habits (insomnia or hypersomnia)	
	Guilt, self-blame	
	Impaired concentration or indecision	
	Suicidal thoughts/ plans/actions	
	Loss of energy/ easy fatiguability	
	Decreased enjoyment/ interest in sex	

Difficulties in diagnosis

Depression can masquerade as, or appear to mimic, a variety of other disorders. Depression in elderly people may mimic dementia, or senility. Dementia is a progressive deterioration in intellectual abilities that results in impaired social and occupational functioning. A person with dementia has a bad memory, and often finds it more and more difficult to think abstractly, to synthesize and learn from new information and to reason logically. The result is poor judgement or inappropriate social behaviour.

In older people, depression can look very like dementia. That is, some of the signs of dementia may be present, but if the underlying depression were to be recognized and treated, the difficulties in memory, judgement and reasoning would decrease or disappear completely. So, in some elderly patients, difficulties with memory and reasoning may be the first sign of a depression.

Other clinicians talk of 'masked depression'. Some patients complain mainly of chronic pain. This may be located anywhere. Pains in the back, chest or abdominal areas are most typical. A careful evaluation frequently reveals the presence of some of the other symptoms of depression. Again, if the depression is recognized, diagnosed and treated, the pains often remit. While anyone may develop a masked depression, studies show that people from non-Western cultures, or from lower socio-economic groups in Western cultures, are more likely to develop such problems.

Depression in children may also be difficult to recognize. Many children develop symptoms similar to those found in adults, but other symptoms may not be so readily identified. One reason why depression may look different in children is that, as the brain matures, child and adolescent go through particular developmental stages. These naturally affect the sorts of signs and symptoms that accompany depression. Difficulties with school-work, lack of enthusiasm and energy, a tendency to withdraw and not play with friends, a tendency to spend more and more time alone, impulsive or angry outbursts, and more than normal 'disobedience' may be the first clues to depression. Both children and adolescents may first express their depressions with 'behaviour problems' such as these. Therefore careful evaluation is needed to find out whether these difficulties are part of the normal growing up pattern or are, in fact, symptoms of depression.

It is not only in the old and young that depression may go unrecognized. Sometimes, depressed adults mistakenly believe they have good reason to be sad and, not realizing that their state is one of more than normal sadness, do not bother to seek help. In fact it hardly matters, diagnostically speaking, whether or not a person can explain why he or she feels sad. The presence of those signs and symptoms shown in the table on page 56 is sufficient to make a diagnosis of depression.

Consider Mr B, a hard-working lawyer, who began to complain of feeling irritable, having trouble sleeping, feeling low in energy, and being concerned over his marriage. He came for help, because his irritability began to affect his behaviour in court. He simply stated: 'I have marriage problems and get anxious about it. I just need some nerve pills.' Not only did Mr B not feel sad, but he had a ready explanation for his nerve problem. However, closer evaluation revealed that a clinical depression had been present for about eight months. His marriage, which had always been a source of some conflict, had deteriorated further, but only after the depressive symptoms had appeared.

Measuring depression

Many people are surprised to learn that the severity of a depression can be easily measured by rating scales that the patient or the clinician completes. Some symptoms of depression may alter according to culture, but it does appear that a core of symptoms persists across cultures. This core of symptoms can be assessed with these rating scales. Two scales illustrate how the severity of a depression can be measured.

The Hamilton Rating Scale is a 17 to 24-item scale that the clinician completes. The severity of the depression is calculated by adding up the score for all

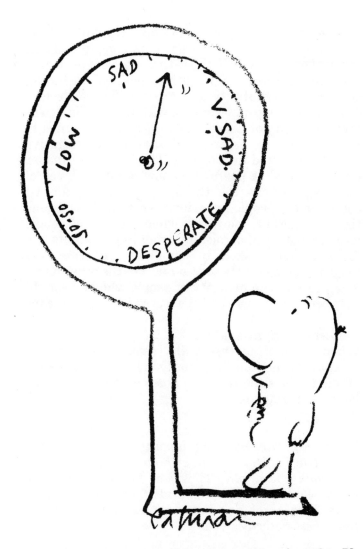

the symptoms, the possible score ranging from 0 to 52. The clinician has to make judgements about such symptoms as depressed mood, guilt, suicidal thinking, insomnia, as well as energy level, feelings of anxiety and bodily pain, etc. This rating scale, which was developed from studies undertaken on British in-patients, has become a world-wide standard in depression research.

Several self-rating scales are also available. These are questionnaires which patients complete themselves. One example is the rating scale below, which tests for a range of negative feelings, including depression, irritability and anxiety. The scale was developed by a group working with Dr R. P. Snaith at the University of Leeds. In essence, it is designed to help doctors to assess the intensity of negative feelings reported by patients. The interested reader may also find it useful to know what evidence of negative feelings the therapist is looking for. Of course, most people experience such feelings at one time or another. However, when a group of people with *no* history of persistent, troubling thoughts and feelings were asked to complete the scale, the majority consistently scored *low*. On the other hand, when tested, the majority of people who had sought help because of such feelings scored *high* on the scale.

Self-assessment scale
When completing this scale, people are asked to accept that the items refer only to their present state of mind. The scale is *not* an absolute measure of any long-term problem.

Please read through the following statements, numbered 1 to 18. How much, or how little, do you think that each one applies to you at the moment? As a guide, each numbered item has four possible variations. Please tick one statement per item which you think best describes you.

Score

1. I feel cheerful.

Yes, definitely	0
Yes, sometimes	1
No, not much	2
No, not at all	3

2. I can sit down and relax quite easily.

Yes, definitely	0
Yes, sometimes	1
No, not much	2
No, not at all	3

3. My appetite is:

Very poor	3
Fairly good	2
Quite good	1
Very good	0

4. I lose my temper and shout or snap at others.

Yes, definitely	3
Yes, sometimes	2
No, not much	1
No, not at all	0

5. I feel tense or 'wound up'.

Yes, definitely	3
Yes, sometimes	2
No, not much	1
No, not at all	0

6. I feel like harming myself.

Yes, definitely	3
Yes, sometimes	2
No, not much	1
No, not at all	0

7. I have kept up my old interests.

Yes, most of them	0
Yes, some of them	1
No, not many of them	2
No, none of them	3

8. I am patient with other people.

All of the time	0
Most of the time	1
Some of the time	2
Hardly ever	3

9. I get scared or panicky for no very good reason.

Yes, definitely	3
Yes, sometimes	2
No, not much	1
Not at all	0

10. I get angry with myself or call myself names.

Yes, definitely	3
Sometimes	2
Not often	1
No, not at all	0

11. I can laugh and feel amused.

Yes, definitely	0
Yes, sometimes	1
No, not much	2
No, not at all	3

12. I feel I might lose control and hit or hurt someone.

Sometimes	3
Occasionally	2
Rarely	1
Never	0

13. I have an uncomfortable feeling like butterflies in the stomach.

Yes, definitely	3
Yes, sometimes	2

	Score
Not very often	1
Not at all	0

14. The thought of hurting myself occurs to me:

Sometimes	3
Not very often	2
Hardly ever	1
Not at all	0

15. I'm awake before I need to get up:

For 2 hours or more	3
For about 1 hour	2
For less than an hour	1
Not at all, I sleep until it is time to get up	0

16. People upset me so that I feel like slamming doors or banging about.

Yes, often	3
Yes, sometimes	2
Only occasionally	1
Not at all	0

17. I can go out on my own without feeling anxious.

Yes, always	0
Yes, sometimes	1
No, not often	2
No, I never can	3

18. Lately I have been getting annoyed with myself.

Very much so	3
Rather a lot	2
Not much	1
Not at all	0

Scoring

The scale is divided into four clusters: add up the scores in each.

Items 1, 3, 7, 11, 15 rate depression
   Score 0—3 rates *low*; 8—15 rates *high*
Items 2, 5, 9, 13, 17 rate anxiety
   Score 0—4 rates *low*; 10—15 rates *high*
Items 4, 8, 12, 16 rate outward irritability
   Score 0—3 rates *low*; 9—12 rates *high*
Items 6, 10, 14, 18 rate inward irritability
   Score 0—3 rates *low*; 8—12 rates *high*

Acknowledgements: R. P. Snaith; British Journal of Psychiatry (1978), 132, 164–71

Many doctors in general practice now use self-rating scales to detect depression and other persistent states of mind that make people unhappy. Such scales are *always* best used in conjunction with skilled professional advice.

5

Different kinds of depression

Grief can't be shared. Everyone carries it alone,
his own burden, his own way.

ANNIE MORROW LINDBERGH (b. 1906)

It is generally agreed that there are different kinds of depression, which is why clinicians now talk of 'affective disorders' in preference to the blanket term 'depression'. Over the last two decades, there has been great controversy as to how 'affective' illnesses should be broken down into sub-categories, and my résumé here represents one current view.

The main division is between the less serious ('normal' and 'situational') depressions and the 'clinical' depressions which require professional help.

'Normal' depression

Sadness is a universal, adaptive response to loss, frustration or stress, and generally lasts for a matter of hours or days. A similar mood change may also accompany specific biological states—for example, many women feel low just before a period.

Returning from a wonderful holiday may also bring on a depressed mood—humdrum everyday life hardly compensates for sun and sand and faraway places. Many people suffer from after-Christmas blues. Such feelings of sadness are quite normal, require no professional help, and are always self-limited. They rarely interfere significantly with one's ability to work, and do not usually cause social difficulties or problems between partners.

Situational depression

Another common type of depression is situational or reactive depression. This state tends to last longer than normal sadness, perhaps weeks or months. Bereavement very often causes this sort of depression, but it could equally well be triggered by other upsetting circumstances. For some women, the post-natal period is particularly difficult.

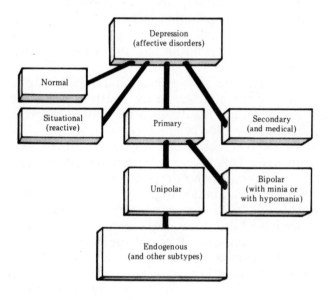

Depending on the situation, this sort of depression may be a quite normal response and may suggest an appropriate awareness of circumstances. Grief, for example, is an understandable response to the death of a loved one. Such a reaction often involves not only sadness, but also some of the other signs and symptoms associated with depression. Often grief gives rise to a number of anxiety-related symptoms as well.

Consider Miss M, a 38-year-old divorced mother of two, who had always been very close to her own mother, especially after the divorce. Her mother became ill and died within a very short period of time. For several months, Miss M experienced intermittent sadness, a general sense of apathy, poor concentration, disturbed sleep and nightmares. She lost her desire to socialize with friends and struggled to keep up at her job. Gradually, however, these symptoms abated. She began to talk to close friends about how unfair it was for her mother to have died so quickly, how alone she had felt and how this event had forced her to re-evaluate her life and the priorities she had set for herself.

Some researchers have found that the interruption of an important attachment by death or separation from a loved one, results in a two-phase response. First, there is a period of protest or agitation, in which feelings of fear, anxiety, anger and restlessness predominate. This phase is then followed by symptoms of depression and despair.

Though situational depressions are common accompaniments of everyday life, they are self-limited and rarely lead the sufferer to seek professional help. This sort of depression does not appear to predispose to clinical depression (a severer form of disorder that requires treatment). There is, however, a modest risk of a situational depression, caused by bereavement, taking on a life of its own and developing into a clinical one.

Secondary depression

The term 'secondary' is used to describe those depressions that arise as a result of another medical or psychiatric illness. Generally speaking, they can be caused in three ways. Firstly, depression can arise as a result of demoralization over the effect that illness or major surgery has on oneself. The cause, therefore, is a psychological reaction to the illness. For example, the sort of patients who may suffer are those with alcoholism, schizophrenia, cancer, neurological damage (e.g., a stroke), people who have had colostomies, mastectomies, burns and plastic surgery and, it has been found most recently, people who have survived heart attacks. Although depressions like these may require professional help, it seems that much can also be achieved through patient self-help groups.

The other two ways that secondary depression can arise are because either the illness itself, or the medication used to treat it, cause chemical imbalances in the body and brain. You could say that this sort of depression has a biological rather than psychological origin. Depressions caused in these two ways are sometimes called medical depressions, though they still fall within the wider category of secondary.

The physical disorders with which medical depression is associated include several endocrine diseases, such as hypo- or hyper-thyroidism, hypo- or hyper-adrenalism, and parathyroid disorders. It may also be brought on by vitamin deficiencies, especially pernicious anaemia (vitamin B12 deficiency), and often follows viral infections such as influenza, hepatitis and glandular fever. Cancer, epilepsy, kidney disease, Parkinson's disease and Huntington's disease may result in medical depression too.

In addition, some relatively uncommon, so-called auto-immune diseases (diseases in which a person produces antibodies which attack his or her own body tissue) may also be associated with this sort of depression. Specific medications which can precipitate depression in those who are vulnerable include those used in the treatment of high blood pressure and other cardiovascular diseases. During medical depression, patients may be taken off particular drugs, otherwise treatment is aimed at the specific physical illness. If the underlying illness is effectively treated, the depression disappears completely in most instances.

It is worth noting that as many as 15 to 25 per cent of those who seek help from a mental health professional may actually be suffering from an underlying and undiagnosed physical illness.

Primary versus secondary depression

Primary depressions are quite different from the normal, situational, and secondary depression we have just been looking at. They occur without a pre-existing or concurrent physical or psychiatric disorder. If bereavement or separation precedes these depressions, the response is clearly out of proportion to these events. In many instances, no such separation is found. Primary depressions are almost always characterized by the full array of depressive symptoms and have many of the attributes of physical disease. If untreated, an episode of primary depression will tend to last six to twelve months, or longer.

Everyone is likely to experience normal depression and possibly situational depression, but only about 15 to 20 per cent of women, and 5 to 8 per cent of men will develop primary depression during their lifetimes.

Often, but not always, a person with primary depression has a history of depression, mania or suicide in the family. Primary depressions are also often associated with a preponderance of bodily symptoms. Specifically, these entail marked disruptions in sleep, appetite and sexual drive; a diurnal mood variation, typically worse in the morning; a complete inability to experience pleasure (technically called 'anhedonia'); a marked slowing down of thinking and behaviour; and, sometimes, menstrual disturbance.

These symptoms and signs reflect a derangement of the centres in the brain which control emotions and appetite, namely the hypothalamus and limbic system. Measuring these biological changes has begun to help us diagnose this type of depression better (see Chapter 6).

A growing body of evidence, and three findings in particular, indicate that there are sub-types of primary depression. Firstly, over the last 20 years, a variety of anti-depressant medications has been developed, and some research suggests that certain primary depressions respond better to one type of drug than another. Secondly, it has been found that some types of primary depression are associated with particular kinds of biological derangements. Thirdly, some primary depressions appear to be more genetically related than others.

Two types of primary depression: unipolar and bipolar illness

From studies of patients suffering from primary depression, two main subtypes have emerged. The first is typified by long episodes of severe depression, accompanied by serious disturbances in normal bodily functions. The second was at one time called 'manic-depression', and involves alternating periods of severe depression and mania. Because severe depression and mania are at the opposite poles of normal human behaviour, these two subtypes have become known as unipolar ('single-poled') and bipolar ('two-poled') depression.

Mania and hypomania

In bipolar illness, episodes of mania are often, but not invariably, separate from the episodes of depression. During a manic episode, a person experiences a distinct change in mood. Typically, he or she feels elated, euphoric or expansive. At other times, an angry or irritable mood may predominate. Associated with this mood change are at least four or more of the following symptoms: being more active than usual; talking more than usual; feeling that one's thoughts are racing ahead so fast that it's difficult to communicate them; having an inflated sense of self-esteem so that you may actually have grandiose ideas or even be deluded about your identity; needing less sleep; being easily distracted (that is, attention is too readily drawn to unimportant or irrelevant external stimuli); and being excessively involved in a variety of activities that you do not recognize as having a high potential for painful consequences. The latter may take the form of buying sprees, sexual indiscretions, foolish business investments, etc. During mania, some people become so out of touch with reality that they experience delusions (fixed false beliefs) or hallucinations. These may be auditory (hearing voices) or visual (seeing things).

These then are the signs and symptoms of mania. They are shown summarized in the table (page 74). It should be said, though, that a number of physical disorders can produce symptoms that might be misdiagnosed as manic. They include tumours or infections in the brain, and endocrine disorders.

Signs and symptoms of a manic episode

General change	Specific changes **Four or more of the following:**	Duration
Mood change, euphoric, expansive, or irritable behaviour— distinctly different from normal	More active than usual	At least one week
	More talkative than usual or a pressure to keep talking	
	Racing thoughts	
	Inflated self-esteem or grandiosity	
	Decreased need for sleep	
	Distractability, inability to concentrate	
	Recklessness, failure to recognize potentially painful consequences of actions (buying sprees, foolish investments, sexual indiscretions)	

A manic episode is relatively short, but should last at least a week in order to be considered a true episode. Mania typically begins suddenly. Symptoms rapidly escalate in severity over a few days. The episode may last for days, perhaps weeks, and it often ends abruptly, sometimes with the onset of a depressive episode.

If this is your MANIC phase – I dread your depressed one...

Sometimes, in bipolar illness it is difficult to distinguish mania from depression. A single episode of illness will meet the criteria for both. Thus, symptoms of mania and depression can be intermixed from day to day, intermixed almost simultaneously, or alternate rapidly every few days.

It is also not uncommon for people to experience spells of hypomania ('hypo' is Greek for 'under' or 'below') between depressive episodes. As the name suggests, this is a less severe form of mania and is experienced simply as a period of unusual energy, great activity and increased creativity. Hypomania does not usually bring the person to medical attention, and it is often not recognized as part of an illness. However, by contrast, the accompanying depressive episodes are often very severe and markedly impair function in occupational, social and personal or marital spheres.

Just to illustrate how disruptive mania as opposed to hypomania can be, let me briefly quote the case of a 42-year-old man who was particularly successful as a surgeon. He had always been known as an outgoing, high-energy type person. One episode of depression struck when he was 35, but only lasted four months and did not lead to treatment, although it badly disrupted his work and his social relationships.

While several hypomanic episodes could be traced back to his twenties, the first manic episode occurred abruptly. He became infuriated with his partner, began to race about the hospital ordering irrational and peremptory changes in the treatment of patients, loudly accusing nurses of siding against him the while. He went without sleep but felt (thankfully) too angry to operate. Instead, he drew money out of his account and flew to Las Vegas to 'relax'. He managed to gamble away nearly $20 000 in several days. After he called his wife for more money and she refused, he began to gamble against credit. After losing to his limit, he became involved in a fight at the casino and was jailed. Only after police and family worked together was he brought to the hospital, still in a manic condition.

Depression in unipolar and bipolar illness

People suffering from unipolar illness will, of course,

only experience depression, whereas bipolar sufferers undergo bouts of depression interspersed with mania or hypomania. In both cases, as we have remarked before, the depression is severe. However, the onset of a depressive episode is variable and not usually so sudden as the onset of mania. Symptoms may develop over a period of days or weeks or, in some cases, over several months. Generalized anxiety, attacks of panic and the development of specific fears or phobias may be seen early in some developing depressions.

About half of those people who develop a single episode of depression will have another one sometime during their life. People with unipolar illness may have single episodes of depression separated by many years of normal functioning. On the other hand, some people experience clusters of episodes, while others report an increased frequency of episodes as they grow older.

How prevalent are unipolar and bipolar illness?

Both types of illness can afflict men and women of all ages and backgrounds. These disorders respect neither culture nor social rank. It is very probable that Napoleon, Abraham Lincoln and Winston Churchill suffered to a greater or lesser extent.

Bipolar illness is equally common in both men and women, and roughly one in 200 adults may suffer this condition. Some research does suggest that bipolar illness occurs more frequently in people with middle- and upper-class backgrounds, and apparently may express itself earlier in life than unipolar illness. By contrast, unipolar illness affects women about two to three times as often as men. Some estimates suggest that 6 per cent of women and 3 per cent of men have an episode of unipolar illness severe enough to require hospitalization.

One important factor that we know predisposes people to primary depression is the presence of the disorder in a blood relative. It seems that this vulnerability is greater where bipolar illness is concerned.

Treatment of unipolar and bipolar illness

Lithium is an element, as silver is, but in its salt form it is a drug which seems uniquely effective in the treatment of bipolar illness. It both reduces the symptoms of mania and prevents the recurrence of episodes of mania and depression. By contrast, lithium does not appear to be as effective an anti-depressant for unipolar illness, although there is evidence that lithium may help to prevent the illness recurring. The tricyclic anti-depressants are successful in reducing depression in both bipolar and unipolar illness, and in preventing depressive episodes from recurring. Electroconvulsive therapy is about 90 per cent effective in treating the depressive episodes of bipolar illness, whereas it is only successful in some cases of unipolar illness during the acute phase. I have summarized all these distinctions in the table below.

Endogenous depression

Finally, we come to 'endogenous' depression. This

Differences between bipolar and unipolar illness

	Bipolar sufferers	Unipolar sufferers
Personal history		
Has episodes of mania or hypomania	Yes	No
Six or more episodes of illness	57%	18%
Mean age at onset of illness	28 years	36 years
Family history		
Depression in blood relative(s)	63%	36%
Suicide in blood relative(s)	Higher	Lower

---

term was originally used to describe any depression which arose without any obvious external cause ('endogenous' means literally 'growing from within'). More recently, the term has been applied specifically to certain types of unipolar and bipolar illness.

We now use the words endogenous or melancholic to describe those depressions which involve severe disturbances in sleep, appetite, weight and sex-drive. Endogenous depression is typically accompanied by a totally unreactive mood which is often at its worst in the early morning. By 'unreactive' we mean the mood is not particularly influenced by day-to-day events or by interaction with other people. The quality of this emotional state is quite distinct from that experienced during bereavement. In addition to this pervasive mood, there is a complete loss of all pleasure, satisfaction or enjoyment.

It is felt by many that endogenous depressions come on very rapidly (over days to weeks). Typically, these episodes can last from three to nine months, although some may go on for a year or two. Finally,

	Bipolar sufferers	Unipolar sufferers
Biochemistry		
Platelet enzyme activity	Decreased	Normal
Red blood-cell enzyme activity	Mildly decreased	Markedly decreased
Physiology		
EEG response to light flashes	Augmenter	Reducer
Treatment response		
Lithium	Good	Fair to poor
Tricyclic antidepressants	Good	Good
Electroconvulsive therapy	Good	Good in some cases

these episodes nearly always end even without treatment, as long as suicide is prevented. However, such episodes often recur.

The physical symptoms of endogenous depression are related to abnormal functions in the pleasure and appetite centres in the brain. These dysfunctions appear to lead to dysfunctions in the pituitary gland, which is the master endocrine or hormone-secreting gland within the brain. These upsets in the pituitary gland are less likely in other forms of depression.

The consequences of primary depression

People who are severely affected by a primary depression may be quite unable to function properly to the extent of being incapable of feeding or clothing themselves, or even maintaining minimal personal hygiene. These sorts of effects are the most serious of the possible repercussions of primary depression. But there are secondary effects of depression and mania which are also significant.

Not infrequently, people who suffer from bipolar or unipolar illness may become dependent on drugs or alcohol, get mixed up in some illegal activity, run into debt, suffer breakdowns in personal relationships, or find themselves involved in divorce proceedings. These are secondary effects of depression. Unfortunately, the underlying cause, namely the depression, may be masked by them, and go unrecognized and untreated.

I recently treated a 52-year-old accountant who had been plagued by a severe alcohol problem for 20 years. During this time he made and lost a great deal of money. He had joined Alcoholics Anonymous in an attempt to treat his drinking problem. It transpired that he had experienced several manic episodes in the past, and a careful look at his history revealed that his excessive drinking was also episodic. Apparently, drinking was his way of trying to control his bouts of mania and depression. I put him on a course of lithium, and soon he no longer felt compelled to drink to intoxication. His alcoholism went into remission along with his bipolar illness.

Depression during adolescence can cause problems at school, ranging from truancy to delinquent behaviour. These difficulties may lead to special counselling programmes, remedial classes, being sent to a special school, or legal action and a spell in a detention centre. Any such action may be quite inappropriate. Failure to recognize a depression can prolong suffering by allowing the person to become even more demoralized and debilitated.

In addition, depression may grossly impair or totally preclude effective occupational functioning. One patient, a 62-year-old construction foreman, took early retirement because, he said, 'I just lost interest in my work'. He sat about his home for three years until his social withdrawal and continued talk of suicide led his wife to bring him to the hospital. History revealed that a severe endogenous depression had been present for a year prior to his retirement. Until then, he had been outgoing, productive and energetic. In retrospect, the depression sapped his interest in everything, which then led to the retirement. After successful treatment, he started a small part-time business of his own, as he said, 'Because I enjoy working'.

Finally, depression may result in suicide. The more hopeless a person feels, the more likely he or she is to attempt suicide. Even if the depression itself is mild, the hopelessness felt can be profound. Tragically, the decision by a depressed person to commit suicide is likely to be based on an unrealistically negative view of the future.

6

What causes depression?

And men ought to know that from nothing else but thence (the brain) come joys, delight, laughter and sports, and sorrows, griefs, despondency, and lamentations . . . By the same organ, we become mad and delirious, and fears and terrors assail us, some by night, and some by day, and dreams and untimely wanderings, and cares that are not suitable, and ignorance of present circumstances . . . all these things we endure from the brain when it is not healthy.

HIPPOCRATES (460–355 BC)

Any discussion of the causes of depression usually involves making a distinction between the 'psychological' and the 'biological'. If we accept that the brain is the organ of the mind then these two terms can be seen simply as different ways of describing the same series of events. So, in matters of mental disorders, we can use the word 'biological' to describe the physical aspects of events going on in the brain, and 'psychological' to describe how those events affect our conscious mind.

Psychological causes

Each of us responds in his or her own way to the same 'objective' event. That is, events acquire a meaning depending on what we have learned, what we value, and what we hope for and expect. So, being fired from a job may make some people afraid, others angry, while still others may breathe a sigh of relief. If we believe that we can never get another job, visions of poverty and deprivation may lead to despair. If we believe that our good work was not recognized or credited anyway, and that being fired testifies to how little we were appreciated, then anger is likely. If the job was a burden to begin with and we had planned to leave but did not know how to announce it, being fired may be a relief. Indeed, we may relish the prospect of new opportunities.

Depending on how we give meaning to an event, or a series of events, we may begin to take a new view of things. This change may be transient or short-lived, but it will influence how we interpret the next series of events. As our thinking changes, so do our brain functions: psychological changes can give rise to biological changes.

For example, say someone very dear to us dies. The love we had for that person is based on an intricate psychological web involving all the events, thoughts and feelings that we experienced which had to do with that individual. His or her death disrupts this deep psychological attachment and is associated with changes within our nervous system. The ensuing grief reaction is characterized by a disrupted sleep pattern that can be measured in our brain waves by an electro-encephalogram (EEG), loss of appetite and weight, and a deep sense of sorrow, longing and despair. We know that appetite and mood are regulated by specific parts of the brain which make up what is called the limbic system. So it seems that events that affect us psychologically can in turn give rise to biological changes in our brain.

The reverse also seems to be true. Biological changes in the brain appear to have psychological consequences. Certain drugs can induce mood changes. Alcohol modifies our senses. As a child physically develops into an adult, thinking styles change, sexual drives are activated and new behavioural patterns emerge.

Factors that produce and maintain depression

Currently, a multitude of theories and ideas are available on how both biological and psychological factors appear to cause or maintain depression. One useful way of thinking about them is to group them into three categories: factors that set the stage for depression (vulnerability factors), those that appear to trigger a depression (precipitating factors), and those that serve to maintain or worsen depression (maintaining factors).

Vulnerability and precipitating factors
Of course, any single factor, such as a bereavement, can be sufficient to cause a situational depression. While no single factor is likely to trigger a severe depression, a combination may begin to tip the balance.

One sort of vulnerability factor is genetic. Research suggests that people who develop manic-depressive (bipolar) illness may inherit changes in the membranes—the outer 'skin'—of certain cells. Scientists are still trying to find out whether cells within the blood, brain cells, or other bodily cells carry this genetic difference. But, as a consequence, it is possible that manic-depressives are particularly sensitive to biological changes, say, those induced by certain drugs or hormonal imbalances.

Factors which cause depression

	Biological	Psychological
Vulnerability factors	Inherited 'leaky' cell membranes	Loss of parent(s) in childhood
	Inherited changes in nerve-cell receptors	Repeated experiences of helplessness in childhood
Precipitating factors	Specific drugs (e.g., Reserpine)	Death of, or separation from, a loved one
	Alcohol	Other losses and stressful events
	Hormone changes	
	Diet	
Maintaining factors	Genetic constitution	Environmental stress
	Biological changes in the brain associated with ageing	Developmental make-up (e.g., negative outlook, demanding value system, learned helplessness)
		Lack of social support
		Lack of social skills

The biological vulnerability factors may mean that these people are particularly vulnerable to depression if they experience psychological upsets such as environmental stresses or losses.

Another kind of predisposing factor can be acquired during early childhood. A single traumatic event, or a series of damaging experiences, such as losses, deaths and separations, can sensitize a child to these sorts of insults in adult life. Similarly, repeated experiences that lead a child to view himself or herself as helpless or ineffective may foster a tendency to give up in the face of obstacles met in adult life. It may be that such childhood experiences lead to changes in the biological functions of the brain so that it cannot respond flexibly to stresses in adult life. At any rate, with this background of vulnerability, factors such as losses or bereavements in adult life may precipitate depression.

Certain factors help to maintain a depression once it has developed. Age, for example, can be a

Im not rejecting you –
I simply don't like
depressed people...

maintaining factor. Certainly, depression becomes more likely in both men and women as they grow older. Of course, this follows the trend of developing an increasing number of physical illnesses as we age.

One specific reason for the age and depression link may be that changes in the chemistry of the brain which take place as we grow older affect the chemicals (neurotransmitters) that communicate between brain cells. As a result the brain finds it more difficult to adapt to stress and makes depression more likely.

Obviously, certain psychological stresses can also help to perpetuate a depression. A string of upsetting events that may just happen to occur during a depression could lengthen it or even make it more severe. Someone who has always found it hard to build relationships may have made few, if any, close attachments. We know that a supportive system of friends and family can help to reduce the impact and intensity of depression: lack of this sort of support very probably serves to prolong depression.

What part does biology play?

We have already mentioned one kind of biological influence which, interacting with psychological causes, can increase vulnerability to depression. It is time to examine such biological causes in more detail.

As we have seen, much research suggests that some people inherit genes which make them prone to developing primary depression. However, although many people may inherit this vulnerability, a great number of them are never actually afflicted. So this suggests that the risk a person runs of developing this sort of depression is influenced by other factors besides genetic inheritance.

The evidence for inheritance

First, let us consider manic-depressive (bipolar) illness. A number of studies involving identical and non-identical twins have suggested that vulnerability can be passed on via the genes. The greater the number of genes you have in common with someone who is a bipolar sufferer, the greater your chance of becoming one too.

Equally, studies which have not involved twins have also tended to bolster the same argument. It seems (though some reports take issue with these findings) that people who have colour-blindness *and* bipolar illness tend to pass on to their descendants a susceptibility to both these disorders. Similarly, it has been shown that a person who inherits the same blood group as a relative who has, or had, bipolar illness runs a greater than normal risk of developing the illness too. We know that the genes for colour-blindness and blood type are carried on the X chromosome, the female sex chromosome, but we do not know how this ties in with the inheritance of bipolar illness.

What is clear, however, is that close blood relatives of people with bipolar or unipolar illness are roughly 13 to 20 times more likely to fall victims to depression than people who are unrelated to a depressive.

One way to separate the influence of learning and development from that of genetic inheritance is to study children of depressed parents who have been adopted and raised by non-blood-related step-parents. Such studies are under way, but have not yet been completed. For instance, the child who is raised by a parent who is frequently depressed may learn to think in negative and depressive ways and learn to respond to stress by becoming withdrawn and depressed.

Biological changes which accompany depression

Significant biological changes occur in association with depression, and the meaning of these changes must be carefully considered.

Firstly, certain biological changes may occur prior to the onset of the depression, that is, before the specific signs and symptoms of depression reveal themselves. These sorts of changes may be clues to the biological causes of depression.

In addition, some changes may simply occur as a result of the signs and symptoms themselves. For instance, people who eat little may salivate less as a consequence, although, obviously, reduced salivation is not something associated solely with depression.

Again, changes may ensue as a consequence of the depression and even persist when the symptoms have disappeared. Such continuing biological changes may act as warnings of a continuing vulnerability to depression.

Finally, some changes are not specific to depression, but can be common to people who have some sort of persistent physical illness. For example, anyone who is relatively inactive as a result of illness other than depression may suffer from constipation and have fewer bowel movements. Similarly, patients who spend a great deal of time in bed with little physical activity may demonstrate changes in their blood calcium levels.

So, although biological changes are present during a period of depression, it does not necessarily follow that these particular changes are characteristic of the depression.

However, certain studies have revealed that three biological changes in particular *are* characteristic of depression, especially primary depression. These are: derangements in the neuro-endocrine or hormone system, particularly in the pituitary gland's response to certain drugs; reduction in the availability of certain chemicals in the brain; and marked changes in the electrical activity inside the brain.

Hormone changes

A hormone is a chemical substance produced, in humans, by various endocrine glands—the adrenal, pituitary and thyroid glands are three examples of endocrine glands. Hormones are carried by the blood to other parts of the body where they can stimulate or inhibit activity. They are, if you like, chemical messengers.

Cortisol is a hormone made by the adrenal glands, which are located above the two kidneys. The rate at which cortisol is produced is controlled by the pituitary gland. This lies beneath the floor of the brain and is often called the 'master' gland because it regulates the function of other endocrine glands.

Early studies showed that some depressions were characterized by over-production of cortisol. At first, it was thought that this hypersecretion simply reflected the stress associated with being depressed. More recent studies have helped us to understand this increased cortisol production rather better. Investigations have revealed that in the most serious types of depression (unipolar and bipolar illness), the adrenal glands often make more cortisol. This is not simply a response to stress. Rather, the extra cortisol is caused by an overstimulation of the pituitary gland, possibly by higher centres in the brain. Studies have indicated that, during a depressive episode, about 40–70 per cent of in-patients with an endogenous depression (whether of a unipolar or bipolar type) show this effect.

Other studies with depressed patients also show derangements in the pituitary's response to other types of chemical challenges. For example, insulin and amphetamine normally stimulate the pituitary to release growth hormone. In people with certain depressions, this growth hormone release is diminished or absent. Furthermore, in some patients, impaired release appears to persist even after the depression goes away. It is possible that a persistent biological change of this sort may go hand in hand with a continuing vulnerability to bouts of depression.

Neurotransmitters

The brain is made up of millions of nerve cells or neurons. These nerve cells are packaged in specific groups, each serving special functions. For instance, the hypothalamus is an area of the brain that regulates appetite, temperature and sexual drive.

It has recently been proved that nerve cells communicate with each other via specific chemical substances called neurotransmitters. Molecules of the neurotransmitter substance are stored in little pockets or vesicles located at one end of each nerve cell. When a cell is activated, it electrically discharges or fires. An electrical impulse then passes along the cell and releases a neurotransmitter at the end of the cell. The molecules of neurotransmitter move across the space (called the synapse) between the nerve cells and attach themselves to receptors on the next nerve cell, causing that cell to fire. After this, the neurotransmitter is inactivated, picked up by the first nerve cell and placed in storage to be used again.

We believe that during depression these groups of nerve cells produce too little of one or more of these transmitter substances. This would result in reduced communication between the nerve cells and account for some of the typical symptoms of depression— changes in sleep, appetite, sexual drive and perhaps mood. Reserpine, and some other drugs that can cause depression, act on these neurotransmitters.

As a result of this evidence, some researchers now talk of different chemical types of depression. Nevertheless, this sort of classification is still controversial.

The sleep electro-encephalogram

The sleep EEG of a normal healthy adult shows that sleep is divided into specific stages. Deep sleep, that is, stage 3 and 4 sleep, is characterized by large, deep waves on the EEG. Most deep sleep occurs at the very beginning of the night, within the first two hours after we fall asleep. At other times during the night, a normal person enters what is called rapid-eye-movement or REM sleep. When in REM sleep, people are likely to have vivid, visual dreams. During this time, their eyes move rapidly and apparently track the visual content of the dream.

The average normal adult has four to five REM or dreaming episodes during the night. The first episode of REM sleep typically occurs about 90 minutes after falling asleep and may last 5 to 10 minutes. As the night continues, the periods of REM sleep recur every 90 minutes and last longer. The last episode of REM sleep may last 20 to 30 minutes, and occurs just before we wake up.

The sleep EEGs of many depressed patients show characteristic changes. During depression, REM sleep comes on much more rapidly and earlier in the night—as quickly as 25 to 60 minutes after falling asleep. Episodes of REM sleep may be more frequent than normal, and a depressed subject will often report that he or she is not only dreaming more, but having

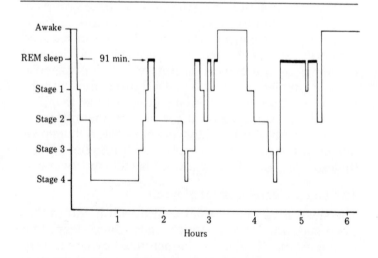

more than usually vivid dreams. In addition, depressed people often obtain much less deep sleep per night than normal. This lack of deep sleep is probably why they do not feel rested after a night's sleep. These sorts of changes are common amongst people with serious depression, and some of them may persist even after the depression has lifted.

The sleep EEG of a moderately depressed patient is shown in the graph on the left. It does not display the specific changes we have just mentioned; it is fairly similar to that of a normal person.

Now look at the graph on the right. This shows the sleep EEG that is typical of primary endogenous depression. Note that the time between falling asleep and the first REM sleep period is quite short. And see how little time is spent in deep sleep, that is, stage 3 and 4 sleep.

What do these sleep EEG changes mean? Well, they are characteristic of primary depressions, particularly endogenous depressions. Without a doubt they show that during depression alterations in brain processes take place. Some researchers go further

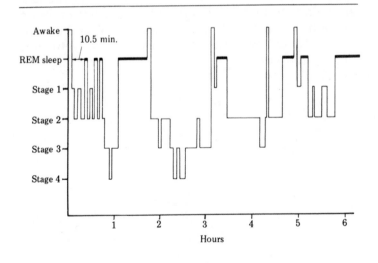

than this and say that the sleep EEG could help us to diagnose different kinds of depression. Others think that the sleep EEG might help us to determine whether or not a particular antidepressant medication will work.

The value of biological measurements

What conclusions can we draw from these biological changes and our measurements of them? Most important, they prove that physiological changes *do* take place in the brain during depression. We know, too, that these changes are specific to depression as opposed to other psychiatric disorders. What is not yet clear is whether these changes are the *result* or *cause* of depression.

Nevertheless, some biological measurements may help the clinician during treatment to monitor its effect. Treatment may reduce the symptoms of depression, but biological tests may still show that all is not normal.

Finally, biological measurements have another valuable role. We can use them to predict the likelihood of depression returning. The sleep EEG and the pituitary's response to certain chemical challenges are being studied for this purpose. Regular monitoring, after depression is apparently 'cured', could allow a doctor to pick up the warnings of returning depression and so prevent the full-blown syndrome developing.

7

Psychological factors

It is not things in themselves that upset us, but
the views we take of them.

EPICTETUS (c. AD 100)

Current stresses and past experiences, and the way in
which they influence our thinking patterns, clearly
have something to do with our vulnerability to
depression. This is not to say that psychological
factors cause all depressions—certainly, they do not
fully account for the development of some primary
depressions. So let us consider some of the ways in
which mental factors may contribute to developing or
maintaining depression.

Grief, anger and self-esteem

Sigmund Freud and Karl Abraham examined mourning or grief as a possible model for melancholia, that is,
depression. They believed that the loss of an important other person, either by death or by disruption,
separation or termination of the relationship, was
related to the development of depression. In their

95

view, people who developed a depression following loss were likely to have ambivalent or mixed feelings about the lost person. That is, consciously they experienced a deep sense of loss at the death of this person whom they valued highly; unconsciously, they had angry feelings towards them. These negative feelings, not available to consciousness, were discharged inwardly. Thus, depression developed as a result of angry, hostile, unconscious feelings that had previously been attached to the other person, but were now directed at the self.

Unfortunately, this 'anger turned inward' theory has gained a degree of popularity not warranted by the scientific data upon which it is based. Quite a few studies have failed to identify increased hostility in depressed patients or increased hostility in their dreams. So it does not appear that depressions as a group can be fully explained by unconscious anger turned on the self.

More recent psychoanalytic thinking has emphasized the role of self-esteem in depression. You can lose self-esteem if someone important to you withdraws their attention or concern. Similarly, your self-esteem may suffer if you lose status or position.

Many depressed people do, of course, view themselves as worthless, helpless and hopeless, but it is not clear that this reduced self-esteem *causes* the depression. In addition, a number of depressed people apparently do *not* have a low opinion of themselves. They simply view themselves as ordinary people who are suffering from a severe impairment in their capacity to sleep, eat, concentrate and function normally.

The influence of 'life events'

The term 'life event' is used by clinicians to delineate anything that happens to us which causes marked emotion. Obviously, the range of life events that fits this definition is immense, and can include desirable things as well as undesirable things. With regard to depression, though, on the whole we are talking about stressful events.

Loss, the breaking of attachments

The British psychologist John Bowlby has emphasized the importance of attachment bondings and loss in depression. Animal studies support this view. It seems that infant monkeys removed from their mothers undergo a period of withdrawal and apparent impairment in social interaction. Certain physiological changes also occur in these monkeys that suggest they develop something equivalent to human depression.

In humans, grief is a response common to all cultures, although the specific symptoms associated with it are highly influenced by the cultural context, sex and age of the grieving individual. Clearly, disrupted attachments precede many cases of situational depression (simply a time-limited grief reaction). However, one study found that a grief reaction developed into a severe depression in about 10 per cent of women in their fifties who had lost their husbands in the preceding year. So, obviously, interrupted attachments can be sufficient to provoke a full-blown depression in a few individuals, while other people simply sustain a situational depression. Whether they are a sufficient cause is not clear. It has been suggested that those people, such as the 10 per cent above, who go on to develop a severe depression, may be genetically or developmentally susceptible to it.

So, if the loss of an important other person does not seem to be a sufficient cause for developing a severe depression, can we say it is a necessary cause? Again, the evidence suggests not. Only 40 per cent of depressed people admitted to hospital report important losses in the six months preceding the illness.

The cumulative effect of stress

Many studies have been done to try and find out if people with mental disorders experience an increase in stressful life events prior to the onset of their problems.

One such study looked at the experience of a group of normal people (living in the community at large) over a two-year period. It was found that, amongst these people, reports of various symptoms, including those of depression, increased or decreased according to the number of stressful life events encountered. Similarly, other researchers interviewed 720 normal adults in New Haven, Connecticut, about their experiences during a three-year period. These people were asked about 62 particular life events and psychiatric symptoms noticed. It was found that a net increase in life events was associated with the worsening of many symptoms, not just depressive symptoms; a net decrease in life events was associated with improvement in symptoms; and the greater the net changes in the number of life events, the greater the change in symptoms. These studies on groups of normal people do suggest that experiencing a large number of stressful events can precipitate various disorders, amongst them depression.

Other studies involved groups of depressed people and control groups of normal people. One found that depressed patients reported almost three times as many life changes as did a non-depressed comparison group. More recently, another found that, compared with a control group of normal, non-depressed people, depressed patients rated life events as requiring considerably more adaptation and change.

These findings show that when depressed people are questioned about life events preceding the onset of their depression, they report that they are under a higher degree of stress compared to non-depressed individuals who experienced the same life events. If two sets of people experience the same sorts of life events, and one set develops depression and the other does not, it implies that factors other than the events themselves contributed to the depression. Thus, it does not appear that an accumulation of life stresses can fully explain many depressions, although they may contribute towards them. However, they may well serve to maintain or worsen the depression once it has developed.

Two researchers have proposed a model to explain the relationship between stressful life events, ongoing vulnerability to depression, and the actual precipitation of an episode of depression. This model relates specific background factors, what a person thinks or makes of what happens to him or her, and the actual events that occur within the six to twelve months prior to the onset of depression.

They suggest that various 'protective factors' help to maintain an outlook based on high self-esteem. Factors such as a high degree of intimacy with one's spouse or partner, and no maternal loss before the age of 11, form the basis for a more consistent, positive outlook and sense of mastery even in the face of various current stresses. By contrast, specific 'vulnerability factors', such as a low degree of intimacy in the marriage, or loss of the mother before the age of 11, may predispose the person to an outlook based on low self-esteem. These vulnerability factors can lead a person to view his or her current interactions with the environment as evidence that he or she is defective.

This piece of research shows that, against a background of vulnerability factors, various 'provoking events' such as losses, threats of loss or continuing long-term difficulties and frustrations will result in grief and a sense of hopelessness. Hence the person is unable to resolve particular difficulties or work through a loss. People who fail to deal with a loss or confront and overcome long-term difficulties begin to avoid solving any situation that presents problems. This avoidance leads to a build-up of further problems, more reduction in self-esteem and a depressive episode.

The study shows, too, that the kinds of symptoms a person develops are also influenced by factors in their past. These factors include the loss of a parent by death or separation, a history of previous depressive episodes, and the age of the individual at the time of the onset of depression.

Other studies support the suggestion that people who develop depression are likely to have suffered the loss of a parent during childhood, while others do not.

Thinking patterns in depression

Other researchers have turned their attention to specific psychological processes present during depression. From this work has evolved a cognitive theory of depression which suggests that some people think about themselves and the world in ways which contribute towards developing or maintaining depression.

Whether cognitive theory can explain the whole spectrum of depression is difficult to say. It may best explain situational depression and some mild to moderate unipolar depressive disorders; we do not know if it can account for bipolar illness or severe endogenous depression.

An accumulation of negatives

Aaron Beck, in particular, has emphasized the importance of cognition or the way we look at the world in depression. He has proposed that three particular thinking patterns are common to depressed people. Firstly, they have a negative concept of self; secondly they interpret their experiences in a negative way; and thirdly they take a negative view of the future.

This idiosyncratic way of thinking appears to revolve around notions of loss and deprivation. Take the concept of self. People who are depressed perceive themselves as deficient, unworthy or inadequate,

because they presume they have mental, physical or moral defects. Adverse experiences and events will tend to be attributed to these defects. They believe they lack the attributes necessary to attain happiness and other important goals.

This negative view of affairs also induces people to misinterpret current and past experiences. They feel the world makes exorbitant demands on them and presents insuperable obstacles that prevent them achieving their life's ambitions. They consistently misconstrue their experiences, and their interactions with others, seeing them as evidence and symbols of defeat and deprivation.

When viewing their future, depressed people anticipate that their current problems will continue indefinitely. If they consider undertaking a particular task, they are likely to expect to fail or fall short of minimally acceptable standards of performance.

Other symptoms of depression can be viewed as consequences of these three negative thinking patterns. Feelings of sadness, loneliness and boredom, lack of energy and ambition, are understandable consequences. For instance, if you think you are being rejected, your feelings will be as intense and real as if you *had* been rejected. Similarly if you believe that failure is inevitable, what reason do you have to make plans and pursue them?

At worst, negative thinking patterns can lead to a suicidal frame of mind. Problems appear both unbearable and insoluble, and suicide offers the only escape. It is actually possible to measure the likelihood of a person committing suicide by gauging the degree of negativity with which he or she views the future.

When even the positive becomes negative

Awareness of this negatively biased thinking can help us understand some of the paradoxes of depression. Remember that it is not a particular life event that determines our emotional response. As Beck has noted, even apparently desirable life events may exacerbate depression.

Consider a businessman who receives promotion after long years of diligent work with a company. He develops a depression following his promotion. It is possible that he may not view the promotion as a reward justly earned. If he has an underlying sense of low self-esteem or incompetence, the promotion becomes a threat or danger. He may think to himself, 'I've been able to get by all these years without having my incompetence discovered. Now that I'm in a position of authority and responsibility, it will be clear to others how little I know about what I'm doing.'

Unrealistic assumptions and beliefs

The cognitive theory also tries to explain why particular people develop depression and how it is maintained. The reason, so the theory says, is that depressed people have learned to make certain assumptions about themselves and the world. They may not be aware of these beliefs, yet all their experiences are interpreted in the light of them. The explanation goes something like this.

Any given situation involves a variety of stimuli. Each individual is selective in the way he or she attends to, organizes and combines these stimuli so that they mean something to him or her. Therefore, specific situations have particular, personal meanings for each of us, and different people will conceptualize the same situations in different ways. However, each of us will tend to be consistent in the way we respond to similar types of events, simply because we have developed our own individual way of thinking about that sort of event. A stable thinking pattern like this is called a schema.

Depressed people, it seems, develop unrealistic schemata. Someone who is over-concerned with whether or not he or she is competent or capable, may implicitly believe: 'Unless I do everything perfectly, I am a failure.' They are therefore likely to interpret situations in terms of competency, even when competence is irrelevant. Let us suppose such a person throws a party. He spends most of the time thinking:

'Is my party up to scratch? Are people enjoying themselves? Will they think I'm a good host?' Instead of enjoying the party, he is anxious and tense, worried about how he appears to others. Preoccupation with an idiosyncratic belief has displaced more appropriate assumptions.

Heads you win, tails I lose

A depressed patient I recently treated at the clinic illustrates how adherence to unrealistic beliefs can cause problems. Mr Samson was in his 40s, and worked as a shopping-mall manager responsible for a large complex of offices and shops. The job paid extremely well, but required that he move every two years. He had recently married for the second time, and was now father of two young children. He complained of various depressive symptoms and was very concerned about earning enough money to cope with inflation. His dilemma was this. He felt committed to his two children and feared that moving every two years would disrupt their development. On the other hand, as the breadwinner in the family, he felt compelled to continue pursuing the high pay associated with the sort of work he was doing. Thus he had two conflicting beliefs: 'I shall have to continue my present job in order to earn as much money as possible,' and 'I must never move again or else it will harm my children's development.' He believed that, if he moved, he would be failing as a father; if he stayed put, his income level would drop and he would be failing as a breadwinner. From his point of view, either way he was a loser, and understandably he felt frustrated, sad and guilty.

His feelings resulted from the two assumptions he had made, and it was only after a lengthy series of discussions that he could accept the possible ways out of his dilemma. Eventually, he agreed that perhaps he could get employment locally which would pay nearly as well as his previous job. He hadn't investigated alternative job options, because he had assumed that he would not find suitable work locally and that his experience would not be respected. It was not so certain either that moving would actually disrupt his children's lives. He had only assumed it would. Intellectually, he had perceived alternatives to his problem, but emotionally he could not be satisfied with any of them until he could be persuaded that one or other of his conflicting beliefs was unrealistic.

Wrong logic

The cognitive theory of depression, as put forward by Beck and colleagues, suggests that the thinking of depressed people demonstrates systematic logical errors. These logical errors involve arbitrary inference, selective abstraction, over-generalization, magnification, minimization and personalization.

Arbitrary inference means drawing conclusions in the absence of evidence to support the conclusion, or even when the evidence runs contrary to it. *Selective abstraction* involves focusing on a particular detail that is taken out of context, while more salient or predominant features of the situation are ignored. The entire experience is conceptualized on the basis of these selectively attended-to details. *Over-generalization* refers to cases where a general conclusion is drawn from a single incident. *Magnification* and *minimization* are errors in evaluation, whereby the relative importance of certain elements in a situation is over- or under-rated. Finally, *personalization* means a tendency to relate external events to the self, when there is actually no basis for making such a connection.

The following example illustrates some of these logical errors. Imagine a secretary who is already somewhat depressed. One day, she types a series of 30 letters. The next day she finds them returned to her desk by her boss. A note is attached to two of the letters asking her to correct a few typing mistakes. To a non-depressed person, this would be part of normal office routine and cause for some annoyance, but that is all. To our depressed secretary this incident may seem far from trivial. She might think to herself: 'I'm a

I'm a Lousy secretary -
I can't TYPE.. I'm a Lousy
EX-Wife and MOTHER..
if I felt any worse
I'd kill myself. I'm so
HOPELESS I'd probably
MESS that up...

failure as a secretary. Everything I do turns out badly.'
As she broods on the situation, she may go on to view
this shortcoming as a reflection of failure in the rest of

her life. 'I'm no good as a mother either; my child is in trouble at school. My ex-husband is not paying the alimony. Everything seems to be going wrong. Since I'm unlikely to achieve anything I want, I might as well kill myself.'

Let us look at this thinking pattern. First of all, she selectively attended to two letters in which there were typing mistakes. She failed to recognize that the other 28 letters were returned without any typing errors at all. Secondly, she over-generalized and over-personalized the experience. She thought there was something wrong with her, namely that she was a poor secretary, overlooking the fact that good secretaries also make typing mistakes. She made only three mistakes in 30 letters, so over 90 per cent of her letters were perfect. Rather than thinking, 'I've made a few typing errors', she construed the return of the letters with their errors as evidence of total personal incompetence. She thought she was defective, not just as a secretary, but as a mother. How can making three typing mistakes have anything to do with being a good mother? She then began to make further negative predictions, assumed that the future held no hope and therefore considered suicide as an escape.

Can other people help?

This whole pattern of negatively biased thinking accounts for the difficulty other people encounter when they attempt to 'talk' someone out of depression. Friends and relatives often try to help the depressed person see alternative, less negative possibilities.

Take the case of someone who is depressed and has recently been fired from his job. A friend might say: 'Why don't you see what jobs are advertised in the paper?' The depressed person responds: 'What's the use of looking? I'll never get what I want.' The friend replies: 'Well, I've just heard about a job that's exactly like the one you lost.' The depressed person might dismiss this possibility without investigating it: 'Well, I'm sure they wouldn't hire me. I'm too old.'

Reassurances by friends may meet a similarly sharp rebuff. Many depressed people will view these assurances as evidence that their friends don't take them seriously, don't understand them or just feel sorry for them. Attempts at comfort or kindness may also be misunderstood as placation or taken as a hint of their incompetence—'I really must be helpless, if you feel you have to help me.'

I am fond of telling the story about a depressed patient who appeared upset one time when I arrived late for her appointment. Of course, when asked what she had been thinking while she waited, she responded: 'I guess you don't want to see me. I'm probably the worst patient you have to face each day.' When I arrived early one day she reported thinking: 'I must be the most severely ill person he has in his practice. Otherwise why would he be spending this extra time with me?' Most of the time I would arrive punctually. Even then she was able to come up with a negative interpretation of the situation: 'He's just running a factory here and doesn't take any personal interest in me.' Hence, whether I came late, on time, or arrived early for her, this patient, while in the midst of her depression, found some way of reading the situation to her discredit.

This sort of behaviour often makes friends or relatives impatient and irritated. They may even begin to blame the depressed person for deliberately self-defeating behaviour. Of course, this negative outlook is not intentional. It is simply part and parcel of depression, just as chest pain is part of a heart attack.

8

Shock and drug treatments

The new always comes in with the sense of violation, of sacrilege. What is dead is sacred; what is new, that is different, is evil, dangerous, or subversive.

HENRY MILLER (b. 1891)

In this chapter I summarize the main medical treatments available today to sufferers from depression. They range from convulsive therapy to salts of the metallic element lithium. In ways that are still to be fully understood, these treatments affect the production, storage and release of various neurotransmitter substances in the brain.

Electroconvulsive therapy

The first modern biological treatment for mental illness, introduced in the 1930s, was electroconvulsive therapy, ECT. ECT has received a poor press over the last 10 to 15 years, a reputation not fully deserved. It is more effective than antidepressants in cases of severe depression, and can be safer than drugs for pregnant women and people with serious heart and other conditions. Nevertheless, it has traditionally been viewed with fear and distrust, and this prejudice seems to linger on.

Early in its history, it was used to treat illnesses, such as schizophrenia, for which it was ineffective. But doctors had no drugs then for psychiatric disorders and, faced with a hopeless case, used whatever treatment was available. The administration of electric shocks at that time was certainly very crude and probably resulted in undesirable side-effects. Nowadays we know how to decide which sorts of depression respond well to ECT, and its administration has been infinitely refined.

How is ECT given?

First, the patient is put to sleep with a short-acting anaesthetic, such as sodium amytal. Next, the patient is injected with another drug which is a muscle-relaxant.

Once the patient is asleep and prevented from moving, an electric current is applied to the right side of the head (unilateral ECT), or is passed from one side of the head to the other (bilateral ECT), by means of electrodes applied to the temples. The current lasts for about 0·1 to 0·5 seconds and induces what is called a 'grand mal' seizure (the same sort that some epileptics suffer). If the patient had not been given a muscle-relaxant, the limbs would initially straighten out and become stiff for about 30 seconds and then move to large jerking motions for about another minute; then the seizure would end. Since the patient is immobilized, these limb movements do not occur. However, the brain still has an electrical seizure, and this can be monitored with an electro-encephalogram.

The seizure is over in about two minutes. Next, the muscle relaxant wears off and the patient wakes up. All in all, the procedure takes about 20 minutes. The patient will then return to the ward or, since ECT may be given to out-patients, return home.

Today, ECT is usually given three to four times

a week, and between five and ten sessions are required for the treatment of severe endogenous depressions.

Is ECT effective?

ECT has been compared to antidepressant medications in many studies carried out beginning in the late 1950s and continuing into the late 1960s. To date, 153 studies, involving 5864 patients, have been conducted. While different research methods were used in the various studies, the mean per cent improvement over all studies gives us a clear picture of whether electroconvulsive therapy is effective in treating depression.

On average, ECT is reported to be effective in some 75 to 90 per cent of patients treated with it. Tricyclic antidepressant medications are reported to be effective in some 60 to 75 per cent of patients treated. A sugar pill or placebo is effective in treating about 25 to 35 per cent of patients. ECT treatment can produce quite dramatic improvement in the patient's condition, and the results are often more rapid than with antidepressants.

Who responds best to ECT?

The sorts of depression most responsive to ECT are those characterized by severe somatic symptoms. These involve severe loss of appetite and weight (greater than 15 lb, or 6·8 kg), marked late insomnia (waking up too early in the morning and being unable to get back to sleep), significant changes in the speed of both thinking and behaviour (psychomotor retardation or agitation), and a mood that is completely unreactive to anything occurring in the environment. In these severe endogenous depressions, ECT may be life-saving. It may even be effective in certain endogenous depressions that do not respond to antidepressant medications.

Let me illustrate the value of ECT by describing a patient we recently treated. Mr Reardon, a 72-year-old, came to our clinic saying, 'I want ECT.' He said

111

that his father had had a history of depression, and at the age of 68 had been given ECT and cured. Mr Reardon had never before, in all his 72 years, been troubled with depression.

In the hope of avoiding hospitalization and ECT, we put him on an antidepressant. He took adequate doses of this drug for three weeks, but he did not respond at all. We stopped this drug and started him on a second antidepressant. This time he developed complications as a result of the drug—he had an irregular heart-beat and had difficulty urinating. So we took him into hospital, gave him a catheter to help him urinate and stopped the second antidepressant medication. A third antidepressant was begun, again in the hope of avoiding ECT. But, once again, he developed complications, and after two weeks had still failed to respond. Finally, all medication was stopped. He was given seven unilateral ECT treatments over two weeks. He responded fully and his depression went into remission. Mr Reardon was then discharged from the hospital and returned to his job as a plumber. We prescribed a low dose of another antidepressant to help prevent a recurrence of his depression. Today, 36 months after ECT, he is fully employed and does not complain of any memory problems.

This case illustrates that treatment with medication is not entirely benign, and that it is not necessarily effective for some patients with severe depression. When Mr Reardon began treatment, he was extremely agitated and distraught. He recurrently thought about suicide as a way to end his suffering. Without electroconvulsive therapy, he might still be suffering or have committed suicide.

The relapse rate following electroconvulsive therapy is about the same as the relapse rate expected after successful treatment with antidepressants is stopped. Within two years, about 18 to 40 per cent of patients who responded to ECT will become depressed again. For this reason, electroconvulsive therapy is used initially to relieve the depression. Subsequently, an antidepressant is often prescribed to prevent the recurrence of depression.

How does ECT work?

The mechanisms by which most medical treatments work are often not clearly understood. This really is the state of play with regard to ECT. We do not know exactly how it works. However, we do know that a convulsion or seizure is essential for the therapeutic effect of ECT. That is, telling people they are going to have ECT, going through the motions, but not turning on the current and therefore not inducing a seizure will not reduce depression. We also know that the seizure modifies the metabolism or turnover of particular chemicals within the central nervous system. Some of these chemicals are suspected in the aetiology or cause of depression.

Is ECT dangerous and what are the side-effects?

Virtually all treatments in medicine have side-effects. The danger of the treatment must simply be weighed against the danger of the illness and the risk that other types of treatment carry.

The aim of a recent study was to find out the comparative mortality rates amongst patients treated with ECT and antidepressants. The investigators did a three-year follow-up survey on a group of patients who had been hospitalized. Some of these patients had received ECT, some had received what was considered to be an adequate dose of antidepressant medication, some received an inadequate dose, and some received none of these treatments. No patient died during any of these treatments. In the three years following treatment, however, it was found that significantly fewer of those treated with ECT had died than either those treated inadequately with antidepressants or those given neither treatment. Amongst those treated adequately with antidepressants, the death rate was comparable to that of those treated with ECT. The overall death rate (both from suicide and other causes) amongst depressives is about two to three times higher than that of the general population. What this study suggests is that ECT reduces the number of deaths that are usually associated with depression.

The side-effects of electroconvulsive therapy are surprisingly few. On the credit side, it must be said that ECT has fewer bad effects on the heart than many antidepressant medications. It can also be given to many people who cannot safely take an antidepressant. On the debit side, effects include a small weight gain and some temporary memory impairment. Long-lasting memory problems are quite infrequent. Recent studies have clearly shown that depression itself impairs certain memory functions. Such memory disturbances are usually improved as a consequence of ECT. Hence, some memory deficiency that appears to follow ECT may result from an inadequate response to treatment.

Immediately after treatment, patients suffer some brief confusion. These problems are most noticeable in the hour or so following ECT. The patient experiences mild confusion and has some difficulty registering what is happening. This follows any seizure, even epilepsy attacks. As more ECT is given, these memory impairments seem to increase. Whether this results from the cumulative effects of seizures, the electricity itself, or the anaesthesia is not known. Typically, these memory problems are mild, fully reversible and last up to a week or two. They are rarely so severe that the person has no memory of what has been going on. Two researchers in particular used a battery of tests to assess specific types of memory in patients six to nine months after ECT. They found no memory impairments in their patients.

The method of giving ECT has been changed in recent years to reduce the possibility of confusion and memory impairments. This new method is called unilateral or one-sided ECT. Here, electricity is administered to only one half of the brain, the right hemisphere. The brain comprises two hemispheres, of which one is called the dominant hemisphere and largely controls language and logic. In most people, this is the left hemisphere. Hence, ECT given to the right side appears to be associated with less memory disturbance than treatment given to both sides of the brain.

Unfortunately, it is true that a number of patients have been given too much ECT, or should never have had it at all, because they had an illness for which ECT is not effective. Over-zealous or inappropriate application of an otherwise effective treatment is obviously a matter of deep concern to both the medical profession and the public. But cases of a treatment being misused are no argument for abandoning the treatment altogether.

Tricyclic antidepressants

These drugs are called tricyclic because they have a three-ring chemical structure. Imipramine, the first tricyclic medication to be used, was discovered in 1957. Since then, other members of the tricyclic family, such as amitriptyline, nortriptyline and doxepin, have become widely available throughout the world.

Amitriptyline   Imipramine

In general, tricyclic antidepressants are administered in gradually increasing dosages until a therapeutic level of the drug in the blood is attained. The patient must then remain on an appropriate dose for at least three weeks in order to obtain the full therapeutic effect.

How effective are tricyclic antidepressants?

These drugs, like ECT, act to reduce or get rid of the symptoms and signs of depression. In successful treatment, a patient's sleep pattern, appetite, weight and sexual drive return to normal. Self-blame, suicidal thinking, indecision and difficulties in concentration are reduced or eliminated. Mood improves and outlook brightens. These drugs also appear to prevent a relapse or recurrence of depression in many people.

The depressions most likely to respond well are those marked by severe loss of appetite and weight, bad early morning insomnia and psychomotor changes (either agitation or retardation). On the other hand, these drugs can also be effective in treating more mild forms of depression. Overall, tricyclic antidepressants produce a therapeutic response in 60 to 75 per cent or more of depressed patients. Of course, the degree of response depends on the dose, the type of drug and the kind of depression it is being used to treat.

The most likely reason for failure to respond to these medications is undertreatment. The doctor may recommend too low a dose, or the patient may fail to take the prescribed amount. These drugs, unlike many other medications, must be taken on a regular daily basis, whether or not the patient feels particularly good or bad at the time. The reason for this is that a constant level of the drug in the blood must be established in order for it to have a therapeutic effect.

How do they work?

The tricyclic antidepressants affect neurotransmitter substances, chemicals which communicate between

116

nerve cells in the brain, especially in the part that controls emotion.

Side-effects

Tricyclic antidepressants are neither addictive nor habit-forming. They are not 'pick-me-ups' or stimulants and do not make you feel 'high'. The side-effects of taking these drugs for a long period of time, even for years, are remarkably few. They may cause mild sedation or sleepiness, and a dry mouth, effects which are worst at the beginning of treatment, but wear off as treatment continues. About 10 to 20 per cent of patients complain of constipation, difficulty in focusing on near objects and shakiness or trembling. But if any of these side-effects are severe, a patient may be given a lower dosage, taken off the drug altogether or put on another one.

Monoamine oxidase inhibitors

Monoamine oxidase, MAO for short, is an enzyme that is found in certain tissues, including the brain. Normally it helps to break down the neurotransmitters involved in the regulation of emotions and appetites. Certain drugs slow down, or inhibit, this process, leaving more neurotransmitters available for communication between nerve cells. These drugs form a group of antidepressants called monoamine oxidase inhibitors, or MAOIs.

As a group, they were fairly widely used before the discovery of tricyclic antidepressants. But today they still have a place in the treatment of some depressions. Two examples of these antidepressants are tranylcypromine and phenelzine.

Choosing the correct dose is a common problem with medications, and MAOIs are no exception. Recently, a blood test has been developed that can help us decide on the best dose for any given MAOI.

How effective are MAOIs?

Specific kinds of depression seem to respond better to treatment with MAOIs than they do to tricyclic antidepressants. But like the tricyclic drugs, MAOIs need to be taken for a number of weeks at the appropriate dose in order to produce a full therapeutic response. Once this response is achieved, MAOIs also seem to assist in preventing relapse.

It has been found that patients with symptoms of acute anxiety, those who are very nervous, tense and unable to relax, often respond well to MAOIs. During depression, these patients frequently develop specific fears or phobias, particularly agoraphobia, which is a fear of being in crowds or in open spaces. Several recent studies have shown that MAOIs are very effective in the treatment of agoraphobia, especially when it is associated with depressive symptoms (it is possible to have agoraphobia without being depressed). In addition, some depressed patients with significant complaints of aches and pains in various parts of their bodies, also do well on MAOIs. These drugs are not as effective if the depression is psychotic, accompanied by hallucinations and delusions.

Side-effects

These drugs should not be mixed with foods rich in a chemical called tyramine. In sensitive individuals, tyramine combined with an MAOI can significantly raise blood pressure. Tyramine-rich foods include certain cheeses and wines, yoghurt and pickled herrings. The list is longer, but any doctor prescribing an MAOI would give the full details.

Lithium

The first person to recognize the potential value of lithium for psychiatric disturbances was John Cade, an Australian doctor. He had found that injecting guinea-pigs with a lithium salt seemed to tranquillize them and make them much less timid. This made him consider its potential in reducing the symptoms of mania. In 1948, he gave lithium to a 51-year-old man who had been in a state of chronic excitement for five years. In his notes, Cade described him as 'restless, dirty, destructive, mischievous and interfering.' He responded dramatically to lithium and was able to go back to work.

It was a long time, though, before lithium became widely used as a treatment for mania, possibly because it was known to have toxic effects. In the USA, it was only approved for the prevention of recurrent manic episodes in 1974.

Lithium is taken daily. Any patient taking a course of lithium treatment starts off with a modest dose. The dose is then gradually increased until the correct concentration of lithium is registered in the bloodstream. This is measured by taking regular blood tests until the lithium reaches the therapeutic level of 0·9 to 1·4 mEq/1 (that is, several hundred times as much as is usually in your circulation). The patient continues to take lithium at the appropriate dosage to maintain this concentration, and the blood lithium level is carefully checked every few months.

Sometimes, lithium is combined with other medications if patients are very disturbed during mania. It is also used in combination with antidepressant medications, particularly in bipolar illness that cannot be controlled with lithium alone. With careful prescription and blood-level monitoring, lithium is a safe and highly effective treatment.

How does lithium work?

Lithium is the lightest known metallic element. We all have it in our bloodstream in very small amounts. The mechanism by which lithium exercises a therapeutic effect is not clearly understood, but there is one mode of action that can be discounted. We know that patients with bipolar depression who respond to lithium are not lithium-deficient. So it seems lithium does not replace lithium missing in the body. The best explanation we have is that lithium finds its way into various parts of the brain where we think it affects the production, storage and release of the neurotransmitters we assume are implicated in depression. However, lithium also changes the function of nerve cell

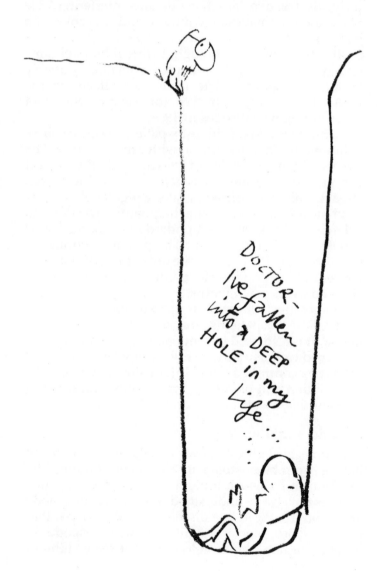

membranes, so it is not absolutely clear whether its therapeutic effect is entirely the result of its action on neurotransmitters.

Side-effects

Lithium is neither addictive nor habit-forming, but it can have some undesirable side-effects. When patients first start to take lithium, they may feel slightly sleepy and may urinate a great deal. These effects wear off as treatment continues. But an excess of lithium can have toxic effects. If a patient has too high a level of lithium in the blood, he or she will experience problems of the digestive system (nausea, vomiting, diarrhoea and abdominal pain); of the central nervous system (slurred speech, staggering gait, mental confusion and memory difficulties); and of the circulatory system (irregular heart-beat due to problems with electrical conduction in the heart). These toxic effects can be prevented by careful monitoring.

A few, relatively rare, long-term side-effects have been reported recently. They include a reduction in the activity of the thyroid gland (hypothyroidism) and changes in other endocrine glands. These effects occur in 1 to 5 per cent of patients. A few recent reports also suggest that lithium may impair kidney function in some patients who have taken this drug for a number of years. In general, though, lithium is surprisingly safe if taken as prescribed and if blood-level concentrations are regularly used to evaluate the dosage.

Newer antidepressants

The next 25 years will very probably see the discovery of various new classes of antidepressants which we hope will be even safer and more effective. They may also allow us to treat some types of depression for which we do not have good treatments at present. Several new antidepressant drugs are already on the market in some countries, and others are being developed. Like the tricyclic antidepressants, they affect the chemical neurotransmitters in the brain, but are designed to act more selectively on particular chemicals. They include the tetracyclic antidepressants, such as maprotiline and mianserin, and other types such as trazodon and bupoprion. All these drugs undergo careful studies for safety and effectiveness. All antidepressant drugs available to clinicians have undergone extensive laboratory and clinical testing.

9

Psychotherapy

Canst thou not minister to a mind diseased,
Pluck from the memory a rooted sorrow,
Raze out the written troubles of the brain,
And with some sweet oblivious antidote
Cleanse the stuffed bosom of that perilous
    stuff
Which weighs upon the heart?

WILLIAM SHAKESPEARE (1564–1616)

Psychotherapy entails an examination of the behaviour, thoughts and feelings related to a failure to cope with or solve problems. Certain ideas or beliefs adopted as a result of early experiences may impair the ability to solve problems, or create behaviour that leads to difficulties. With help from a therapist, depressives can learn to assess their beliefs objectively, and reject those thinking patterns that make them depressed.

Psychotherapies range from the sort commonly used by many professionals to some fairly unusual types of treatment, the efficacy of which has not been demonstrated. Some may help to relieve depression, others might even make it worse. In this chapter, my main focus is on what is called cognitive therapy, an approach which seeks to change negative patterns of thinking in the patient which may serve to maintain, as we have seen, certain forms of depression. Cognitive therapy has proved effective in treating a variety of non-clinical depressions. It can, of course, be used on its own or combined with drug treatment. Other forms of psychotherapy may also help depression.

The cognitive therapy approach

Cognitive therapy is based on the premiss that a person's emotional response to situations is determined by the way he or she thinks about them— 'thinking' in this instance meaning all those thoughts, verbal representations and pictorial images of which the person is consciously aware. These develop as a result of previous experiences, and come to form consistent patterns of beliefs which then determine the way in which that person reacts to new situations.

Treatment is short-term, usually involving a maximum of 20 sessions spread over 10 to 12 weeks. During treatment, the therapist takes an active, directive role. The treatment follows a logical, graduated plan, somewhat like an educational course, and provides the patient with a series of highly specific learning experiences. During treatment the patient learns to:

(a) recognize and record automatic negative thoughts;

(b) recognize the connections between thinking patterns, emotions and behaviour;

(c) examine the evidence for and against particular distorted thoughts;

(d) substitute more realistic thinking for irrational or unfounded negative thinking;

(e) identify and then change beliefs that lead to negative distortion of experiences.

Unlike the therapist in more traditional therapies, the cognitive therapist continually and deliberately interacts with the patient and structures the treatment in order to engage the patient's participation and collaboration. The more severe the depression, the more actively the therapist structures and directs the

treatment. The patient, helped by the therapist, reviews his or her thoughts, inferences and conclusions to see if they are realistic, logically consistent, reasonable. They are tested one at a time to determine whether they are valid or invalid.

Depressed patients are initially often confused, preoccupied or distracted. So the therapist starts off by helping them to organize their thinking and behaviour, so that they can begin to cope with the immediate demands of everyday living. Treatment focuses on current rather than past problems. Little attention is paid to childhood recollections, except to clarify the basis of present thinking about events. In contrast to classical behaviour therapy, cognitive therapy places more emphasis on the patient's internal non-visible experiences, on thoughts, feelings, wishes, daydreams and attitudes.

Almost every daily experience provides an opportunity to investigate the patient's negative views or beliefs. For example, if a male patient reports that other people constantly seem to be turning away from him, or taking no notice of him, the therapist will help him to design a method for evaluating other people's reactions. This helps the patient sort out whether the facial expressions, bodily movements and verbal comments of others actually indicate rejection, or whether he is reading rejection into situations in which other explanations are more likely.

To take another example, this time of a patient who believes she is incapable of carrying out simple personal hygienic tasks such as washing her hair or brushing her teeth: the therapist might help her devise a checklist or graph to record the necessary steps involved in looking after herself.

'Graded task' assignments

In depression, the cognitive therapist's aim is to relieve symptoms such as apathy, self-criticism and thoughts of suicide. One of the techniques commonly used is the graded task assignment, designed to raise patients' self-esteem by providing them with a series of success experiences. These serve to combat attitudes expressed as 'I can't do anything', or 'Everything I do turns out badly.'

The graded task technique is often used with patients who have difficulty completing quite simple tasks that were previously no problem. Though someone may have the skills and information needed to perform a task, he or she may find it almost impossible to carry out while depressed. They may not even attempt to do so; they feel defeated before they even try.

A graded task assignment entails breaking down a complex task into a series of small intermediate steps, which the patient is encouraged to undertake one at a time. I say 'complex' task, because many of the everyday chores we perform almost automatically involve a fair amount of organization and self-confidence that we take for granted.

Example of a graded task

Let us imagine we are designing a graded task for a depressed housewife, Mrs Jones, who finds herself unable to do her food shopping. We encourage her to list the specific tasks involved in shopping: first, she needs to make a list of the groceries she wants; then she needs to walk to the shop or get there by car or bus; then she will have to enter the shop, take the goods from the shelves and pay the cashier for them; then she will have to walk, drive or take transport home; finally she will have to unload her shopping and put it away in the appropriate cupboards.

Severely depressed patients are sometimes unable to accomplish a complete series of steps. What stops them? The answer is that as they take the first step, in the case of Mrs Jones making a list of the items needed, they are then bombarded, or rather bombard themselves, with thoughts of making inappropriate decisions. They anticipate criticism from others along every step of the way. Compiling a list of the steps involved serves to make them aware of such negative thoughts.

To return to Mrs Jones, she may believe that no matter what she decides to buy and cook the family will moan and criticize. Using logical discussion and reassurance, the therapist would help her to examine objectively the possible consequences of buying and preparing something the family might not like. Would *all* members of the family not like it? Have they ever refused to eat because of these preferences? What foods are least controversial? Does it desperately matter if someone doesn't like a meal?—he or she doesn't have to eat it. The therapist would help her see that making a decision about what to buy is more important than trying to please everyone.

Next, she is persuaded to go to the shop and return home without actually going inside. As she approaches the shop, new negative thoughts may loom, thoughts such as 'They probably don't have what I've got on my list', or 'I'll never be able to find everything I need', or 'I probably don't have enough money to pay for everything on my list.' This series of thoughts betrays the tendency, characteristic in depression, to anticipate a negative outcome when there is no objective evidence to support that view.

As our lady undertakes this phase of her graded task assignment, her negative outlook on the future becomes the target of more logical discussion and objectively based revision with the therapist. She is helped to consider alternative plans of action, should she actually encounter one of these anticipated obstacles. What items on the list are essential? Are there acceptable alternatives for some of them? Having an alternative plan ready can dispel concern over an anticipated problem.

Over a period of time, Mrs Jones would plan and then execute each of the steps involved in shopping. With each step she would test her assumptions about obstacles, about other people's reactions to her behaviour. Each step would become a stimulus for re-evaluation of those assumptions, with the help of the therapist. As she manages each step needed to accomplish her overall goal, she begins to feel less helpless, more competent, more self-esteeming. She may begin to think: 'Perhaps I *can* do the shopping. Obstacles don't exist everywhere. I am anticipating more difficulties than is realistic. If I put my mind to it, and take one step at a time, I can begin to cope, at least in small ways.' Her outlook brightens. With this improved sense of accomplishment, she may consider tackling other tasks, such as cleaning the house. In this way, she learns to confront and accomplish tasks that she had come to assume were impossible.

There's nothing like a LIST for making a person feel ORGANISED...

The Triple Column Technique

This is another approach used in cognitive therapy. It is called the Triple Column Technique because it deals with assessing the relationship between three things: events, thoughts and feelings. The depressed patient is encouraged to write down events, thoughts and feelings during times when his or her mood worsens. With help from the therapist, he or she can then objectively evaluate the thinking patterns involved and understand how they are related to feelings and actions. This can help to reduce guilt and self-criticism.

Let me illustrate this technique by describing the case of Mr Paul Stotus. Before his depression, Paul had been a successful electrical engineer and a responsible breadwinner for his family. During his depression, he became highly self-critical, and nearly every waking moment would think to himself how little he was accomplishing and how he was letting his family down. He had already learned in previous therapy sessions to identify and record his stream of negative thoughts.

To help him recognize the stereotyped nature of his thinking, the therapist asked him to record specific events and associated thoughts that had occurred whenever his mood plummetted. This written record revealed that Paul found grounds for self-criticism whatever the event. The next step was to urge him to become engaged in one or two activities that would help him realize how he under-rated his accomplishment and magnified his deficiencies. The next week, he recorded that he had wallpapered his neighbour's kitchen. Immediately afterwards, he began to feel much more depressed. He even started to think of suicide again.

When asked what thoughts he had about this event, he said he had thought, 'I did it all wrong. It looks terrible.' Further discussion revealed that he had wallpapered the kitchen almost single-handed. His neighbour was actually very pleased with the job, even though Paul was severely disappointed with it and therefore depressed.

The therapist, not surprisingly, felt that wallpapering a kitchen would be quite an accomplishment, even for someone who was not depressed. Yet Paul saw his wallpapering effort as a failure. Why? How bad a job had he done? Did it need redoing? Was his neighbour upset or critical? Had someone laughed at his effort? Nothing of the sort had happened. Apparently, the wallpaper had a flowered design on it, and Paul reported that the pattern was misaligned. However, his neighbour had not noticed the misalignment. In fact, no one but the patient had noticed it. How badly matched was the pattern?

To get an objective report, his wife, Arlene, was brought into the session. She said that she was not aware that the flowers were misaligned at all. Arlene was quite surprised that she had not noticed the fault. After detailed questioning, he admitted that in some of the panels there was a discrepancy of about two millimetres. A two-millimetre misalignment was all the evidence he needed to conclude that he was personally inadequate and incapable of doing anything, even something as simple as wallpapering a kitchen! After this discussion, and once he realized that his wife had not even noticed the error he thought was obvious, Paul began to understand how harshly he had misjudged himself. Perhaps he was using unrealistic criteria to judge his own behaviour. Had he always judged himself so harshly?

Several such incidents were recorded and evaluated. A recurrent theme ran through many of these reports. It was as if Paul believed: 'Unless I do everything perfectly, I am useless as a person.' In fact his excessive self-criticism had turned obvious successes into abysmal failures. How could this self-critical tendency be changed? Was it really true that personal value was so closely tied to successful accomplishments? Was perfection a realistic goal?

As a further step to help Paul evaluate himself more realistically, the therapist proposed a series of 'homework assignments' designed to reinforce self-esteem. These were tasks that would help him realize that what he accomplished was the product of chance, skill, and effort. He could not be expected to control chance completely, nor could he be expected to be exceptionally skilful at everything. And if, after having made a reasonable effort, results were not perfect, this could in no way be a reflection of total personal failure. He had to be made to realize that, in fact, very worthwhile people often make mistakes.

These mistakes do not diminish their overall worth, although they do serve to remind us that all human beings have their limitations.

Therapy for couples

For a number of reasons, the partner or spouse of a depressive patient may be asked to take part in therapy. Very often, he or she can act as a valued objective reporter. As we saw in the case of Paul, his wife was instrumental in getting him to reappraise a situation in which he felt he had failed. However, some marriages or close relationships may inadvertently reinforce certain maladaptive beliefs that predispose to depression. Just to give you an example of this, take the following case, where communication between a couple breaks down unintentionally.

A depressed wife asks to go shopping. Her husband agrees, but starts to work on another project in the home. He feels happy and thinks, 'I'm glad she's feeling good today. I'll finish this job and then we'll go shopping.'

While he is working at the task, she begins to feel angry. (Remember that irritability is typical of depression.) She thinks, 'First he promises to go shopping and then he lets me down. He doesn't really care.' (Note how she has read rejection into the situation.) Next she withdraws to the bedroom, while he continues to work. Her sadness increases as she thinks, 'Nobody really cares about what I want. I don't really deserve to go. He has more important things to do. I shouldn't make demands on him. I'm too selfish.' (She has become self-critical and has discounted her own importance to her husband.)

Meanwhile, her husband becomes nervous as he notices that she has retreated to the bedroom. He begins to think, 'She's going into one of her moods again. I wonder what upset her? I'd better leave her alone or she'll lose her temper.'

Later, he decides to make dinner to take the pressure off her. After he has prepared the meal, she becomes more sad and tearful, thinking, 'He doesn't even need me to do things in the house any more. The kids didn't even notice that I wasn't around. I'm totally worthless to my family.' Finally, her husband becomes irritated and stalks out, thinking, 'Well, if she's going to pout all night, I'm going out for a beer.'

This kind of interaction can only exacerbate the situation. Yet it is commonplace, because depressed people have difficulty in taking an objective view of situations and in sharing their inner thoughts and feelings.

Does psychotherapy work?

Several recent studies have shown that cognitive therapy, and a few other psychotherapies, are effective for some depressed patients, particularly those who are outpatients. Indeed, in two outpatient studies, psychotherapies that emphasize changes in behaviour or thinking have been shown to exceed the effects of antidepressants. Both studies also showed that fewer patients prematurely gave up psychotherapy than drug treatment.

Another outpatient study found that interpersonal psychotherapy, another short-term structured treatment specifically designed for depressions that focuses on role changes and interpersonal behaviour, equalled the effects of antidepressant treatment. One recent report also suggests that cognitive psychotherapy helps to prevent depression recurring after treatment is discontinued, in contrast to antidepressants, which have no preventive effect after the medication is stopped. Whether in fact particular psychotherapies provide protection against relapse is a matter requiring, and receiving, further study. Promising though these early findings are, they cannot be accepted unreservedly. In addition, for some sorts of depression medication is clearly needed, whereas in other sorts of depression psychotherapy may be preferable.

Self-help methods

What can be said of self-help techniques for depression? Well, it is best to tackle the problem by copying the approach adopted in cognitive therapy. Try to make yourself assess the situation objectively. Don't personalize what is happening. Don't make generalizations from single events. Don't jump to conclusions. Consider alternative ways of viewing problems. Anticipate success as often as failure—there is no reason to expect one to be more likely than the other. Anticipate obstacles, but make contingency plans. Talk to friends and relatives to get another opinion, a different view. Be aware of self-critical thinking and fight it. Making a mistake suggests corrective action

may be needed; it doesn't imply personal inadequacy. Look at the assumptions you are making about particular situations and about other people. Are these assumptions accurate? Are you sure? How do you know?

There is little evidence yet that self-help is effective once depression becomes severe. On the other hand, it may be useful either in preventing a full-blown depression from developing, or in reducing the length of some situational depressions. The hallmark of a depression that requires professional help is that you cannot talk yourself out of it. Seeking that help is a sign of wisdom, not of weakness.

10

What to do when depression strikes

He who conquers others is strong;
He who conquers himself is mighty.

LAO TSE (c. 604–531 BC)

Nobody is immune to the experience of depression. Primary and secondary depressions constitute a large category of undiagnosed medical and psychological problems that significantly interfere with important aspects of people's lives, and may end in suicide. So, it is vital to recognize depression when it occurs, and seek professional help when it is needed.

Is your depression serious?

Let us recap the four major subdivisions of depression. First, there is sadness, a normal mood, and part of everyday life. It may last a few hours, possibly a few days. It may be associated with specific life events, such as separation from or loss of a loved one, or with complex psychobiological states, such as the menstrual cycle. These periods of normal sadness are time-limited, associated with recent life events, and do not interfere with personal relationships or one's capacity to work.

Secondly, there are situational depressions. Although they last longer, usually weeks or months, they are akin to normal sadness and are an appropriate reaction to painful events. They are time-limited and can easily be related to specific life events in time and intensity. Full recovery is expected if the stressful situation is removed, and as time passes. Grief, due to loss or bereavement, causes this kind of depression. Symptoms of a situational depression include a mood disturbance, mild difficulty with sleep (especially sleeping more, rather than less), a small change in appetite and a very modest change in weight. Job performance and personal relationships may suffer briefly, but to no great extent.

Support from friends and family and applying a few self-help methods may be all that is needed in many situational depressions. Professional assistance is usually not required. However, should self-examination, discussion with others, and the passage of time fail to alleviate a situational depression, the possibility of a major depression must be considered. Remember, that in a situational depression, self-esteem is generally maintained, even though feelings of loneliness or sadness may be acute. The sufferer does not believe that he or she is personally defective. Delusions, hallucinations and suicidal intentions rarely, if ever, accompany benign situational depressions. And generally they should not last longer than three or four months.

The third category is secondary depression. This can be more severe than the situational kind, and may require treatment. It can accompany physical or psychiatric illness, either as a result of the illness itself, or because drugs used to treat the illness have produced chemical changes in the body or brain. Secondary depressions, whether physically or psychologically caused, may be helped with professional care.

The fourth kind of depression, which is usually

severe enough to require professional intervention, is primary depression. Signs and symptoms involve a mood change; significant changes in sleep pattern, appetite, and weight; increased feelings of guilt; suicidal thinking; changes in speed of thought and behaviour; decreased sexual interest and an incapacity to enjoy the usually pleasurable things in life. If these symptoms persist for more than a month, or if they interfere with day-to-day functions, professional help is necessary.

A primary depression often has an autonomous, self-perpetuating course that may last for months. Not infrequently, one or more relations will have had depression as well. People who suffer bouts of hypomania or mania interspersed with periods of depression are suffering from bipolar depression.

It should also be remembered that secondary problems may make it difficult to recognize primary depression. Symptoms such as impotence, inability to reach orgasm, palpitations, extreme sweating, diarrhoea, nausea, vomiting, menstrual disturbances, or chronic pain can mask an underlying depression. Overworking, drinking too much, or failing at your job can also be consequences of depression.

Helping yourself

Self-rating depression inventories that identify and measure the signs and symptoms of depression can help you to decide how bad your depression is, and whether you should seek help. The Beck Depression Inventory, shown on pages 60 to 63, is one such self-rating scale. People who are free of symptoms score 0 to 9. Those with mild depression score 10 to 18. A score of 19 to 25 designates a moderate depression, 26 to 35 moderate to severe. Severe depressions score 36 and over. But you need to be a little wary of these self-reports, because they are not diagnostic instruments and cannot replace a doctor's full medical and psychological evaluation. Various physical disorders, a normal grief reaction, and self-limited situational depression can elevate scores on this test.

Let us assume that you have recognized the signs and symptoms of depression. Try to evaluate your current circumstances and how you interact with other people. Are there situations that you have been ignoring that could, in fact, be frustrating you or making you feel hopeless and helpless? Are your relationships with other people less satisfying than they were? Do you find yourself wanting to avoid people, wanting to withdraw socially? Are you becoming more suspicious of other people's behaviour and less trusting of your own judgement? Are previously smooth-running relationships, perhaps with your family or at work, more difficult than they were?

Friends and family are often important sources of information when you are trying to assess whether symptoms are present and, if so, their severity and possibly their cause. Choose someone who knows you on a day-to-day basis. Has he or she noticed any change in your behaviour, in your mood, in the way you look, in your general zest for life? Do they feel that you have somehow become less involved in everything, more self-critical, more withdrawn, less trusting? Sometimes another person can recognize links between particular events and the changes in your behaviour that you may not have been aware of.

After careful assessment of specific symptoms, your current life circumstances, and changes in personal relationships, try to decide whether this is a normal 'down' or a situational depression, both of which should be self-limiting and disappear without professional intervention. Normally, feeling 'down' only lasts a few days, and a situational depression should not persist longer than three or four months. If what you are experiencing fits neither bill, then possibly you are suffering from a secondary or primary depressive illness for which professional assistance is required.

Self-diagnosis beyond this point can be dangerous. If the signs and symptoms that you have identified are compatible with either secondary or primary depression, seek professional help. Even if you are not sure, go and get a professional opinion. The first, and most important, step in seeking professional advice is to *make an appointment with your doctor*. If necessary he or she will be able to refer you to a specialist for a further opinion.

Escaping from a situational depression

What techniques might help in self-limited situational depressions? A few general points are worth making. First, giving up and doing nothing appears to be more detrimental than attempting to do something. Secondly, an objective reappraisal of your self, your future, and the world around you, facilitated by

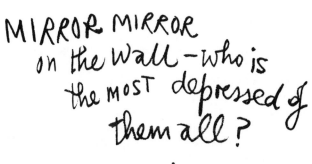

discussions with friends and relatives, may be helpful.

Thirdly, if there are conflicts between yourself and other important people in your life, such as bosses, employees, children, spouses or partners, these conflicts should be directly confronted and aired. An objective and dispassionate attempt to solve problems can be useful. Discussions between the aggrieved parties in which disagreements are outlined, preferences stated, areas of collaboration sorted out, and ways of negotiating differences chosen, begin to solve and reduce specific conflicts.

Finally, you may be confronted with a situation that forces you to revise your values, beliefs and ideals pretty dramatically. Sometimes this can be accomplished without professional help, but it can be made easier with experienced professional assistance.

As an example of this, let me quote the case of a patient who recently suffered the loss of one of her three children in a fire. Her children had been her primary investment in life. Her role as a mother and homemaker was vital to her self-esteem, although she was also a loving wife and contributed a great deal to the community. She had generally assumed that if, as the mother, she did all that was in her power to appropriately raise and protect her children, then obviously nothing bad would happen to them.

When one of her children died in a fire, this woman suddenly began to realize that her children, in spite of all her magnificent efforts, were just as vulnerable as any of us to disappointment, injury, and even death. She blamed herself for her son's death. She doubted her ability as a mother and became self-critical of her life in general. She could no longer see any value in raising her other children and being a mother. She felt that all that she did was basically meaningless. She saw her children and herself as victims of a hostile, unpredictable, and unforgiving world. As she began to wonder whether anything was worthwhile, she emotionally withdrew from her remaining children, her husband and the community.

The fire and death of her son had shattered her previous values and beliefs. This forced her to reconsider what was of importance in her life. She was unable to settle back into her previously established roles, but her self-doubt made it difficult for her to adopt new roles. Over several months, following the tragedy, she tried to reorganize her life, revise her priorities, and cope with day-to-day responsibilities as best she could. Her family and husband were very supportive, as were a number of close friends who offered assistance and a sympathetic ear.

However, as time passed she continued to be plagued with self-doubt and persistently lacked energy. Vivid pictures of the fire kept going through her mind, and environmental stimuli unrelated to the fire became triggers that brought to mind the death of her son and her self-doubt. What had been a situational depression was developing into a primary affective disorder.

She attempted to cope through a series of self-help manoeuvres. She talked to her friends, tried to get involved in community activities, tried to assist her remaining children with homework and be interested in their progress at school, and so on. But these self-help efforts did not succeed. After several months, she realized that professional help was needed. The treatment she received was the kind of cognitive therapy we outlined in Chapter 9. As treatment progressed, she began to reorganize some of her beliefs about herself and the world, to accept the tragedy emotionally. She has now picked up the threads of her life again. There is no knowing, of course, whether she would have pulled through eventually without professional help. But one thing is fairly certain: her depression would have lasted longer, and possibly deepened, and had more serious repercussions on those around her, if she had not sought expert help.

References

Chapter 2

Adams, F. (ed. and translator), *The Genuine Works of Hippocrates*. Baltimore: The Williams and Wilkins Co., 1939.

Beck, A. T., Brady, J. P. and Zuen, J. M., The history of depression. *Psychiatric Annals*. New York: Insight Communications Inc., 1977.

Siegal, R. E., *Galen on Psychology, Psychopathology and Function in Diseases of the Nervous System*. Basel: S. Karger, 1973.

Chapter 3

Kendall, R., Relationship between aggression and depression: epidemiological implications of a hypothesis. *Archives of General Psychiatry*, 1970, 22, 308–318.

Lyons, H., Depressive illness and aggression in Belfast. *British Medical Journal*, 1972, 1, 342–344.

Marsella, A. J., Depressive experience and disorder across cultures. In: Triandis, H. and Draguna, J. (eds), *Handbook of Cross-Cultural Psychology, Volume 5: Culture and Psychopathology*. Boston: Allyn and Bacon (in press).

Murphy, H. B. M., The advent of guilt feelings as a common depressive symptom: a historical comparison on two continents. *Psychiatry*, 1978, 41, 229.

Pfeiffer, W., The symptomatology of depression viewed transculturally. *The Transcultural Psychiatric Research Review*, 1968, 5, 121–123.

Tan, E. S., The presentation of affective symptoms in non-western countries. In: Burrows, G. D. (ed.), *Handbook of Studies on Depression*. Amsterdam: Excerpta Medica, Elsevier, 1977.

Chapter 4

American Psychiatric Association, *Diagnostic and Sta-*

tistical Manual of Mental Disorders, third edition, Washington, 1980.

Beck, A. T., A systematic investigation of depression. *Comprehensive Psychiatry*, 1961, 2, 163–170.

Beck, A. T., Rush, A. J., Shaw, B. F. and Emery, G., *Cognitive Therapy of Depression*. New York: Guildford Press, 1979.

Ekman, P., Friesan, W. V. and Ellsworth, P., *Emotions in the Human Face*. Elmsford, New York: Pergamon, 1972.

Hamilton, M., A rating scale for depression. *Journal of Neurology, Neurosurgery and Psychiatry*, 1969, 72, 201–205.

Lesse, S., *Masked Depression*. New York: Jason Aronson, 1974.

Sutherland, S., *Breakdown*. Weidenfeld and Nicolson, 1976.

Chapter 5

American Psychiatric Association, *Diagnosis and Statistic Manual of Mental Diagnosis*, third edition, Washington, 1980.

Angst, J., *Zur Ätiologie um Nosologie endogenen depressiven Psychosen*. Berlin: Academie-Verlag, 1966.

Fieve, R. R., Rosenthal, D. and Brill, H. (eds), *Genetic Research in Psychiatry*. Baltimore: Johns Hopkins University Press, 1975.

Flach, F. F. and Braghi, S. G. (eds), *The Nature and Treatment of Depression*. New York: Wiley, 1975.

Klein, D. F., Endogenomorphic depression: a conceptual terminological revision. *Archives of General Psychiatry*, 1974, 31.

Parker, C. M., *Bereavement: Studies of Grief in Adult Life*. New York: International Universities Press, 1972.

Chapter 6

Akiskal, H. S., A biobehavioral approach to depression. In: Depue, R. A. (ed.), *The Psychobiology of the Depressive Disorders: Implications for the Effects of Stress*. New York: Academic Press, 1979.

Akiskal, H. S. and McKinney, W. T., Jr., Overview of recent research in depression: integration of ten conceptual models into a comprehensive clinical frame. *Archives of General Psychiatry*, 1975, *32*, 285–305.

Carroll, B. J., Neuroendocrine functions in psychiatric disorders. In: Lipton, M. A., Mascro, A. D. and Kellam, R. F. (eds), *Psycho-pharmacology: A Generation of Progress*. New York: Raven Press, 1978.

Carroll, B. J., Curtis, G. C. and Medels, J. Neuroendocrine regulation in depression II; discrimination of depressed from non-depressed patients. *Archives of General Psychiatry*, 1976, *33*, 1051.

Carroll, B. J., Feinberg, M., Greden, J. F., Tarika, J., Albiala, A. A., Haskett, R. F., James, N. M. I., Krontrol, Z., Lohr, N., Steiner, M., de Vigne, J. P. and Young, E., A specific laboratory test for the diagnosis of melancholia. *Archives of General Psychiatry*, 1981, *38*, 15–22.

Dorus, E., *et al.*, Genetic control of lithium transport across the red blood cell membrane; relationship between cell membrane function and the etiology of affective disorders. In: Obrols, J., Ballus, C., Gonzales, M. E., *et al.* (eds), *Biological Psychiatry Today*. New York: Elsevier, North Holland Inc, 1979, 1143–1147.

Fieve, R. R., Rosenthal, D. and Brill, H. (eds), *Genetic research in Psychiatry*. Baltimore: Johns Hopkins University Press, 1975.

Flach, F. F. and Braghi, S. G. (eds), *The Nature and Treatment of Depression*. New York: Wiley, 1975.

Kupfer, D. J., REM latency: a psychobiological marker for primary depressive disease. *Biological Psychiatry*, 1976, *11*, 159.

Ostrow, D. G., Gyanshyam, N. P., Davis, J. M., Hurt, S. W. and Tosheson, D. C., A heritable disorder of lithium transport in erythrocytes of a subpopulation of manic-depressive patients. *The American Journal of Psychiatry*, 1978, *135*, 1070–1078.

Perris, C., A study of bipolar (manic depressive) and unipolar recurrent depressive psychoses. *Acta*

Psychiatrica Scandinavia, 1966, 42, Supplement 194.

Schildkraut, J. J., The biochemistry of the affective disorders: a brief summary. In: Nicholi, A. M., Jr., M.D. (ed.), *The Harvard Guide to Modern Psychiatry*. Cambridge, Massachusetts: Belkrap Press of Harvard University, 1978.

Schildkraut, J. J., Orsulak, P. J., Schatzberg, A. F., Gudeman, J. E., Cole, J. O., Rohde, W. A. and LaBrie, R. A., Towards a biochemical classification of depressive disorders. I. Differences in urinary excretion of MHPG and other catecholamine metabolites in clinically defined subtypes of depression. *Archives of General Psychiatry*, 1978, 35, 1427.

Scott, J. P. and Seray, E. C. (eds), *Separation and Depression*. Washington DC: American Association for the Advancement of Science, 1973.

Winokur, G. and Cadoret, R., Genetic studies in depressive disorders. In: Burrows, G. D. (ed.), *Handbook of Studies on Depression*. Amsterdam: Excerpta Medica, Elsevier, 1977.

Chapter 7

Beck, A. T., *Cognitive Therapy and the Emotional Disorders*. New York: International Universities Press, Inc., 1976.

Bowlby, J., The making and breaking of affectional bonds. I. Aetiology and psychopathology in the light of attachment theory. *British Journal of Psychiatry*, 1977, 130, 201.

Brown, G. W. and Harris, T., *Social origins of depression: a study of psychiatric disorders in women*. New York: Free Press, 1978.

Myers, J., Lindenthal, J. and Pepper, M., Life events and mental status: a longitudinal study. *Journal of Health and Social Behavior*, 1972, 13, 398–406.

Myers, J., Lindenthal, J. and Pepper, M., Life events and psychiatric impairment. *Journal of Nervous and Mental Disease*, 1971, 152, 149.

Parkes, C. M., *Bereavement: studies of grief in adult life.* New York: International Universities Press, 1972.

Paykel, E. S., Myers, J. K., Dierelt, M. N., Klerman, G. L., Lindenthal, J. J. and Pepper, M. Life events and depression—a controlled study. *Archives of General Psychiatry*, 1969, 21, 753.

Rush, A. J. and Beck, A. T., Cognitive therapy of depressions and suicide. *American Journal of Psychotherapy*, 1978, 32, 201–219.

Schless, A. P., Schwartz, L., Goetz, C. and Mendels, J., How depressives view life events. *British Journal of Psychiatry*, 1974, 125, 406.

Chapter 8

Avery, D. and Winokur, G., Mortality in depressed patients treated with electroconvulsive therapy and antidepressants. *Archives of General Psychiatry*, 1976, 33, 1029.

Crow, T. J. and Johnstone, E. C., Electroconvulsive therapy: efficacy, mechanism of action and adverse effects. In: Paykel, E. S. and Copper, A. (eds), *Psychopharmacology of Affective Disorders.* Oxford: Oxford University Press, 1979.

Hollister, L. E., *The Clinical Use of Psychotherapeutic Drugs.* Springfield, Illinois: Charles C. Thomas, 1973.

Jefferson, J. W. and Griest, J. H., *Primer of Lithium Therapy.* Baltimore: Williams and Wilkins, 1977.

Kalenowsky, L. B., Electric and other convulsive treatments. In: Arieti, S., Freedman, D. X. and Dyrud, J. E. (eds), *American Handbook of Psychiatry.* New York: Basic Books, 1975.

Kline, N. and Angst, J., *Psychiatric Syndromes and Drug Treatment.* New York: Jason Aronson, 1979.

Scholl, M., Special review: lithium in psychiatric therapy and prophylaxis. *Journal of Psychiatric Research*, 1978, 6, 67.

Squire, L. R. and Chace, P. M., Memory functions six to nine months after electroconvulsive therapy. *Archives of General Psychiatry*, 1975, 32, 1557.

Chapter 9

Beck, A. T., Rush, A. J., Shaw, B. F. and Emery, G., *Cognitive Therapy of Depression*. New York: Guildford Press, 1979.

Kovacs, M., Rush, A. J., Beck, A. T. and Hollon, S. D., Depressed outpatients treated with cognitive therapy or pharmacotherapy. A one-year follow-up. *Archives of General Psychiatry*, 1981, *38*, 33–39.

McLean, P. D. and Hakistan, A. R., Clinical depression, comparative efficacy of outpatient treatments. *Journal of Consulting and Clinical Psychology*, 1979, 47, 818–836.

Rush, A. J., Beck, A. T., Kovacs, M. and Hollon, S., Comparative efficacy of cognitive therapy and pharmacotherapy in the treatment of depressed outpatients. *Cognitive Therapy and Research*, 1977, *1*, 17–37.

Weissman, M. M., Prusoff, B.A., Di Mascio, A., *et al.*, The efficacy of drugs and psychotherapy in the treatment of acute depressive episodes. *American Journal of Psychiatry*, 1979, *136*, 555–558.

Index